TWELVE
GATES

WHERE DO THE NATIONS ENTER?

First Fruits of Zion is a 501(c)(3) registered nonprofit educational organization.

First Edition 2012
Printed in the United States of America

ISBN: 978-1-892124-66-1

Cover Design: Avner Wolff
Cover Illustration: Drake "The Drake" Dunaway

Quantity discounts are available on bulk purchases of this book for educational, fundraising, or event purposes. Special versions or book excerpts to fit specific needs are available from First Fruits of Zion. For more information, contact www.ffoz.org/contact.

First Fruits of Zion

PO Box 649, Marshfield, Missouri 65706–0649 USA
Phone (417) 468–2741, www.ffoz.org

Comments and questions: www.ffoz.org/contact

Boaz Michael
Through writing, speaking, and creative vision, Boaz has served the faith community for 20 years. Boaz is the founder and director of the ministries of First Fruits of Zion and Vine of David, which are leading voices in Messianic Judaism. The educational missions of both ministries challenge the status quo of today's Church and also the Jewish views of Yeshua (Jesus). To find out more about Boaz you can visit his ministry website at www.ffoz.org or his personal blog at www.boazmichael.org.

TWELVE GATES

WHERE DO THE NATIONS ENTER?

BOAZ MICHAEL

*It had a great, high wall, with twelve gates,
and at the gates twelve angels, and on
the gates the names of the twelve tribes
of the sons of Israel were inscribed …*

(Revelation 21:12)

CONTENTS

INTRODUCTION

The search for the "Ten Lost Tribes of Israel" has been part of Western civilization since its Christianization. Legends about the lost tribes have inspired people for thousands of years. Theories as to their identity and location have been offered by historians, rabbis, scholars, and researchers of every stripe. During the Age of Exploration, as the known world expanded, many explorers sought with eager anticipation to find the lost tribes across the next river or mountain range, through the next forest or jungle.[1] Surely, it was thought, they must exist—but where?

This sense of mystery and excitement surrounds the legend of the lost tribes to this day. Like the search for the Ark of the Covenant or the Holy Grail, immortalized in dozens of novels and films, the search for the lost tribes evokes images of ancient scrolls, secret maps, and lost records.

There is an influential view in the Hebrew Roots movement, called variously "Ephraimite" or "Two-House" theology, which capitalizes on this sense of wonder. Ephraimites believe that modern Christians may be the descendants of the ten lost tribes.[2] This idea is at first inspiring and intriguing. Many newcomers to the Hebrew roots movement have happened upon this idea and now think that they must be attracted to the feasts, customs, and laws of Israel because they are really Israelites, direct descendants of the northern tribes which were exiled over 2,700 years ago.

This realization, if true, would be laden with prophetic significance. Many end-time prophecies pertain to the Jewish people. The twelve tribes, for instance, are prophesied to come together as one body and to inherit the land of Israel in Ezekiel 37:15–28—the ingathering of the exiles. Could it be that modern Christians have a share in that inheritance? Are Christians about to be gathered to the promised land to live alongside the Jewish people? Should they be moving to Samaria? Furthermore, the children of Israel, according to Romans 9:4, inherit the "adoption to sonship; theirs [is] the divine glory, the covenants, the receiving of the law, the temple worship and the promises."[3] What a glorious and enviable calling!

This idea—the idea that modern Christians are in reality descendants of the ten lost tribes—is at the core of the Two-House movement. Its followers call themselves Ephraimites, after Ephraim, one of the names given to the Northern Kingdom of Israel. It's easy to understand why Two-House theology is so popular. The idea that people who are attracted to the Hebrew roots of our faith are actually biological descendants of Abraham, Isaac, and Jacob, and therefore entitled to the promises of God, is inherently attractive. If this idea is true, it gives Gentile[4] believers in the Hebrew roots movement an ancient, concrete identity, and a basis for their relationship with God that appears to have impressive continuity with the Old Testament. It also casts the entire movement in a prophetic light; prophecies pertaining to the Jewish people can, in this framework, be applied to modern-day Gentile believers.

The emotional and apocalyptic appeal of Two-House theology is also strong. For example, Revelation 21:12 describes New Jerusalem as having twelve gates named after the twelve tribes of Israel. On that basis, many Two-House proponents advocate the idea that only Israelites will enter into God's presence there. Consequently, in many Two-House circles, "Gentile" is a dirty word. All believers must be "Israel." Those who adopt Two-House theology along with its "Israelite" identity may even feel like they are entering into God's family for the first time.

Imagine a child who was adopted at a very young age. When he grows up, he might yearn to know his biological parents. Though he has been fed, clothed, and cared for by a loving mother and father for his entire life, the knowledge that his real ancestry, his real history, lies somewhere else is almost too much to bear.

Suppose that in the course of life he hears a rumor that he is descended from royalty and is heir to a great fortune. He will certainly leave behind his adoptive family in search of his biological parents and the fortune that awaits him. In the same way, many Ephraimites have left mainstream Christianity behind and practice a form of Judaism under the auspices of their claimed identity as biological children of Abraham, Isaac, and Jacob. Many of them believe they are destined to inhabit the land of Israel along with the Jewish people,[5] and that they are to keep the commandments of the Mosaic Law.[6]

To be sure, the Two-House movement shares many affinities with Messianic Judaism. Both affirm basic Christian doctrines such as the deity of Jesus Christ as well as traditional Messianic beliefs such as the continuing relevance of the Torah (the Mosaic Law) and the prophetic role and significance of the Jewish people. Many Two-House proponents, as a result of their affinity with both Judaism and Christianity and their intense respect for the Scriptures, live to a high ethical standard and are known for their moral purity and acts of kindness. This work is not meant to denigrate them or their religious practices.

Nevertheless, there are issues with Two-House theology, issues that bear serious consideration by Messianic Judaism and by the rest of the Hebrew roots movement. These issues will be explored in the rest of this booklet. Chapter one is a brief history of the legend of the ten lost tribes and the birth of modern-day Messianic Judaism as the foundation of the Two-House movement, a history of the movement itself, and an overview of its distinctive traits. Chapter two examines the Scriptural evidence for Two-House theology. Chapter three introduces other (non-textual) issues with Two-House theology. Chapter four introduces an alternative to Two-House theology, a theology of Gentile identity and inclusion in the "commonwealth of Israel" based on the Scriptures and on the most recent scholarship.

I am indebted to my young friend Jacob Fronzak who researched, drafted, and revised this booklet based upon my previously published paper, *Encounters with an Ephraimite*.

CHAPTER ONE

A HISTORY OF THE TWO-HOUSE MOVEMENT

You've probably heard the story of David and Goliath. Thousands of years ago David, a young Israelite boy with a ruddy complexion, slung a stone at the giant Goliath, and by the power of God, the rock sunk into Goliath's forehead and killed him. This same boy went on to be the ruler of Israel, uniting all twelve tribes under his rule in Jerusalem. After his death, one of his sons, Solomon, inherited the throne, and for a while he did well. He was very wise. He expanded Israel's territory. He even built the Holy Temple.

But Solomon had a problem—a lady problem. He had a thousand wives and concubines from many foreign nations, with some of whom Israel was forbidden to intermarry, and many of them continued to worship their ancestral gods. According to 1 Kings 11, Solomon's wives led him astray into idol worship, turning his heart after other gods. God appeared to him twice to warn him of his anger and impending judgment, but Solomon continued down the path of idolatry. Consequently, as an act of divine judgment, Solomon's kingdom was divided after his death. His son Rehoboam lost control over all of the tribes except for Judah (and Benjamin, which by that time in history had largely assimilated into Judah).[7] According to 2 Chronicles 11:13–15, the tribe of Levi also migrated down to the Southern Kingdom from their ancestral cities in the north. So three tribes remained under Rehoboam's rule.[8]

The other ten tribes (remember, Joseph's was split in two—Manasseh and Ephraim—making a total of thirteen) were ruled by

Jeroboam. Jeroboam made idols for the citizens of the Northern Kingdom to worship and instituted a new priesthood in place of the Levitical priesthood. The Northern Kingdom never recovered from this descent into idolatry. God repeatedly urged her to return to him, and promised to judge her unless she repented, but she would not listen. After a few centuries, she was finally conquered by the Assyrians and her citizens were deported.

The Ten Lost Tribes

The Scripture is not clear about what happened to the deported Israelites from the Northern Kingdom. It does not contain a specific record of the corporate return of the northern tribes such as it does for the return of the remnants of the Southern Kingdom of Judah in the books of Ezra and Nehemiah.[9] Centuries passed, and later readers wondered what had happened to them. As a result, legends formed to explain their seeming absence from the biblical record and from history. Speculation developed about their supposed travels from the lands to which they were deported by the Assyrians east to the Orient or west into Europe, or perhaps across the sea. But as these lands were explored, the identity and location of the lost tribes remained a mystery.

Time passed; explorers rounded the globe; the tribes remained lost; and the myths grew more extravagant and more intricate. Legends of the ten lost tribes fascinated Christianized Europe. Even the great rabbis of the time joined in the speculation. Since it seemed that the whole world had been explored and the tribes had still not been found, some speculated that they must have lost their identity. Subsequently, widely disparate people groups, from the Japanese to the Native Americans to the Anglo-Saxons, were offered as descendants of the lost tribes.[10] Most of these theories didn't gain much lasting traction, though a variation on the Native American theory found its way into the Book of Mormon.[11] The Anglo-Saxon theory, however, proved to be remarkably popular, and became known as "British Israelism" or "Anglo-Israelism."

Gentile Identity Crisis

Fast-forward to the 1970s. The Hebrew Christian movement, until then a missionary enterprise designed to make Christianity look attractive to Jews, began to reflect on its identity and purpose in ways that previously had been unthinkable.[12] In 1975, the Hebrew Christian Alliance of America changed its name to the Messianic Jewish Alliance of America, signifying a shift in practice away from traditional Christianity and toward a full-fledged form of Judaism.[13] These Messianic Jews were, of course, still believers, and they remained orthodox in their doctrine, but they had rediscovered their distinct identity as Jews. To reflect this newfound identity, they began to worship in "Messianic synagogues" instead of "Hebrew Christian churches." They met on Saturday instead of Sunday. They sang songs in Hebrew.

This Messianic Jewish revival wasn't limited to the Jewish people. Many Gentile Christians found themselves attracted to the movement as well. After all, Jesus himself, a practicing Jew, observed Jewish holidays like Passover and Tabernacles, kept the dietary laws, and wore fringes on his garment. What better way to experience a connection with Jesus, it was thought, than to imitate his actions? How better to understand him than to study the Jewish context of his life and teaching?

The large numbers of Christians who seek to explore the Jewish religious and cultural context of Jesus' teachings and those of his apostles have become loosely known as the "Hebrew Roots movement." Within that broad definition there exists today a wide variety of beliefs and believers, including current and former members of the Worldwide Church of God and its offshoots; Messianic Jews who are not affiliated with mainstream Messianic Judaism; mainstream Christians; Ephraimites; and many others, some of whom have simply dropped out of church life and begun meeting in homes.

Hebrew Roots advocates almost universally reject supersessionism (the idea that the church has replaced the Jewish people and that the Mosaic Law is done away with). However, supersessionism was a large component of the classical answer to the Gentile question—that is, how can Gentiles benefit from the covenants God made with the Jewish people without becoming Jewish? The rejection of supersessionism raised questions of identity: If the

Jews are still God's chosen people, what about believing Gentiles? Do they become Jewish? If not, then what?

For many people, these questions remained unanswered. Meanwhile, with the shift from Hebrew Christianity to Messianic Judaism came a mentality that the movement was, like any other form of Judaism, just for Jews. Gentiles who had attached themselves to the movement began to feel marginalized as they were told that the Torah and Jewish tradition were not for them. This was despite the fact that many of these Gentiles were extremely devout, and some even held themselves to a high standard of Torah observance informed by rabbinic tradition—in some cases, more so than the Messianic Jews with whom they were fellowshipping.

The author of a pamphlet published by a Two-House organization laments the fact that to become a full member of the Messianic Jewish Alliance of America, one must be Jewish; Gentiles can only become "honored associate members."[14] It goes on to allege (without providing a source) that hundreds of thousands of Christians who were attracted to Jewish customs but were not allowed to participate as Jews in Messianic Judaism consequently gave up their faith and converted to (non-Messianic) Judaism "to be equal to the Jew."[15]

This desire—the desire to be equal to "the Jew"—implies the basic assumption that Jews have a status more honorable than that of Gentiles in the body of Christ, an assumption warranted by the seemingly exclusive nature of Messianic synagogues. However, this is not the case, nor does any reputable Messianic organization teach that Jews are in any way superior to Gentiles.[16] This issue will be addressed in chapter four.

The Two-House Movement

Many ministries offered answers to the identity issue. Some of these answers were no different from the classical Christian understanding. Others tried to formulate new theologies of Gentile inclusion in Israel that affirmed the continuing role of the Jewish people. Two-House theology emerged as a strong, though variegated, solution. At its core, the proposed answer was simple and elegant: Gentile Christians who were attracted to the feasts, laws, and customs of Israel might just be descendants of the ten lost tribes. Their inclination to practice a form of Judaism might in fact be genetically stimulated.

This answer seemed to tie up all the loose ends and put everyone on equal footing. Not only had an ancient mystery been solved, but Gentile Christians attracted to Messianic Judaism could claim that they had just as much right as Messianic Jews to practice a form of Judaism alongside the Jewish people. These "Ephraim-ites," as they called themselves, could read the Old Testament as directly applying to them, since they were physical descendants of Abraham, Isaac, and Jacob. They could expect to see the ancient prophecies about Israel's re-gathering and restoration fulfilled, not only in the Jewish people but in themselves as well. On top of that, an apocalyptic, millennial eschatology brought an "end-times" fervor to the movement.

This new theology attracted a large number of followers, which only served to confirm the apocalyptic expectations of the move-ment. Today its representatives can be found nearly anywhere there is a gathering of Hebrew Roots advocates.

Many years ago, a young Two-House teacher told me that "the Two-House movement is the valid alternative to that of the Mes-sianic Jewish movement." He based this statement on the fact that the Messianic Jewish movement had rejected Gentiles who desired to embrace a life of Torah. He explained that the single valid alterna-tive to living in a community connected with other Torah-keeping, non-Jewish congregations is to accept the understanding of the Two Houses of Israel.[17]

This was essentially the formative impulse of Two-House the-ology. It is an alternative to Messianic Judaism, a movement that gives Gentiles a presumed Israelite status as a basis for adopting a Jewish style of worship.

Initially, First Fruits of Zion, though skeptical as to Two-House claims, reached out to the Two-House movement. At no small expense, we attended many conferences where Two-House theol-ogy was prevalent in an effort to build bridges with the Two-House community. In 2003, I wrote a white paper called *Encounters with an Ephraimite* in which I pushed for reconciliation and mutual understanding.

FFOZ's former "One Law" position made the issue of ancestry immaterial; we could advocate along with Two-House teachers the idea that non-Jewish believers were obligated to all of the commandments in the Mosaic Law, albeit for different reasons. We were not proponents of Two-House theology, but neither did we set ourselves against it.

When our position changed from "One Law" to that of "Divine Invitation,"[18] and we could no longer advocate the imposition of the Mosaic Law as a covenantal obligation on Gentile believers, we were broadly rejected by the Two-House movement. Position papers were written against us and we found ourselves unwelcome at conferences. Our relationship with the Two-House movement came to a screeching halt.

This work represents, among other things, a reevaluation of the Two-House movement's theology from a more authentically Messianic Jewish perspective, which embraces the historic identity of the Jewish people and the importance of Jewish tradition in preserving that identity and in remaining faithful to the covenantal obligations of the Jewish people.

Two-House Theology

As stated above, Two-House theology is variegated. Any monolithic description of its theology is bound to marginalize some and offend others. There is no central authority that can be cited, nor is there a shared doctrinal statement that can be analyzed. However, a few core works have gained widespread acceptance within the Two-House movement. One of these is Batya Wootten's *Who Is Israel?* published in 1998. A short overview of her work's distinctive traits, with a few interpolations from other Two-House sources, will suffice to introduce the reader to the basics of Two-House theology.[19]

First, the core of Wootten's Two-House theology is the theory that large numbers of modern Gentile Christians are descendants of the ten lost tribes. Though Wootten is careful not to limit the possibilities of Israelite descent in racial or ethnic terms,[20] she hints that Ephraimites would exist in "the West,"[21] possibly a reference to Europe and America.[22] One does not have to go far into the movement to find those who go even further, locating "Ephraim" almost exclusively in the Anglo-Saxon nations. The parallels between these teachers and advocates of British Israelism like Steven M. Collins and Yair Davidiy are noteworthy and will be explored further in chapter three.

Second, due to the Ephraimites' proposed ancestry, Wootten implies that they are obligated to obey the commandments of the Mosaic Law.[23] This is not a legalistic, works-based form of salvation; accusations that Two-House theology is legalistic[24] are just as unfounded as the same allegations when leveled against Messianic Judaism. However, the desire to be "Torah-observant" as a response to the saving grace of God to some degree characterizes the entire Hebrew Roots movement, and Two-House theology is no exception.

It must be observed, though, that "Torah observance" as defined by the recipients of the Torah— the Jewish people—is totally irrelevant to most Two-House teachers. From a Jewish perspective, no one in the Two-House movement is in reality Torah observant. Many commandments, like *tefillin* and the particulars of *kashrut* (such as the purity of ceramic vessels or the removal of the sciatic nerve, both recorded in the Torah), are generally ignored as extra-biblical rabbinic injunctions or reinterpreted.[25] Other commandments, like Sabbath observance, are observed in some sense but with no connection to the historical Jewish method of their observance.

Furthermore, "Torah observance" in a Two-House context invariably prescribes the same exact requirements for Jew and Gentile. Drawing on texts like Exodus 12:49 and Galatians 3:28, Two-House teachers advocate "one law" for all believers, thereby erasing any halachic distinction between Jew and Gentile/"Israelite."[26]

Third, on the basis of Ezekiel 37:15–28, Wootten argues that Ephraimites and Jews will be reunited as one body in the land of Israel.[27] This reunification and occupation of Israel is described in military terms, with an "invincible army" fighting against the "Philistines."[28] She is presumably referring to the Palestinians.[29]

Fourth, Wootten does not accept the traditions of rabbinic Judaism.[30] She describes a Christian fascination with Jews and Judaism as jumping "out of the frying pan and into the fire."[31] She accuses Judaism of, among other things, changing the Biblical calendar,[32] and, importantly, she rejects Judaism's definition of who is and is not Jewish.[33] Repudiation of Rabbinic tradition is quite common in the Hebrew Roots movement, but for Wootten, this rejection is necessary in order to substantiate her claim that modern-day "Ephraim" must be accepted as the descendants of Israel along with the Jewish people. The implications of this viewpoint are explored further in chapter three.

Finally, Wootten advocates leaving behind mainstream Christianity. She likens Christian holidays to the idolatrous practices instituted by Jeroboam and sees a direct correlation between the apostasy of the ancient Northern Kingdom and their supposed successors, the Gentile Christian Church.[34] Her references to "muddied waters" and "errant shepherds" are unmistakable references to Christian doctrine and Christian pastors; her call to "leave behind" such things can only be interpreted as a call to leave the church.[35]

This short overview of Two-House theology and its origins is hardly comprehensive. Then again, to go into more detail would only paint an unrealistic picture of an organized, coherent body, something the Two-House movement is not. The essential common element to all Two-House advocates is the identification—tentative or dogmatic—of modern Gentile believers with the descendants of the lost tribes of Israel, and it is this core tenet of their theology that will be examined in the next chapter. We will find that although there may be descendants of the exiles who have assimilated into Gentile culture, the Scriptures and other historical texts do not support the idea that their descendants can make a claim on Jewish/Israelite identity or the idea that such a claim can or should form the basis for a theology of Gentile identity in the *ecclesia*.

CHAPTER TWO

AN EXAMINATION OF THE TEXTUAL EVIDENCE FOR TWO-HOUSE THEOLOGY

Like any other canonical narrative[36] of the Scriptures, Two-House theology has its own way of pulling together elements from the large number of books and passages of different genres in the Bible so that they tell a smooth, coherent story across both Testaments. The focus of this story, from a Two-House perspective, is the dispersion of the ten lost tribes 2,700 years ago and their rediscovery at the end of time to herald the return of the Messiah and the ingathering of the exiles.

This narrative employs several major themes that are emphasized in the Scripture, particularly the ingathering of the Jewish exiles, the reconstitution of the nation of Israel, and the return of Israel to a state of blessing and obedience. The twist is that these themes are speculatively applied to modern-day believers who have no verifiable genetic or historical connection to the Jewish people.

Evidence for this reading of the Scripture is taken from the Old Testament, the New Testament, and other historical writings. Each of these sources will be considered in turn. While a complete survey of the evidence is beyond the scope of this short work, a sampling of Two-House proof texts and exegetical methods will suffice to introduce the reader to the core problems with Two-House theology.

A Multitude of Nations

Two-House theology relies heavily on the theory that large numbers of modern-day believers are descended from the ten tribes which formed the Northern Kingdom of Israel until they were exiled by the Assyrians c. 721 BCE and deported to distant lands, where they intermingled and intermarried with the inhabitants of other nations and lost their identity as Israelites. This theory has several anchor points in the Old Testament, "proof texts" that supposedly point forward to the identity of Ephraim, or the Northern Kingdom, being tangled up with a large number of Gentiles. One of these verses is Genesis 48:19, in which Jacob blesses his newly adopted son, Ephraim, saying, "His offspring shall be a multitude of nations (*ve-zar'o yih'ye m'lo ha-goyim*)."

The Hebrew word *goyim* is commonly used in the Scriptures themselves and in later Jewish literature to refer to non-Jews. It is often translated in these contexts as "Gentiles." On that basis, Two-House teachers believe that Jacob was prophesying that Ephraim's descendants would literally become a multitude of non-Jews or non-Jewish nations. In this vein, Wootten translates the phrase "*m'lo ha-goyim*" as "a fullness of Gentiles." [37]

It's not as simple as it sounds, though. Hebrew words, like English words, have a range of possible meanings. Not every meaning applies in every case where the word is used. For example, the English word "heart" can refer to the organ that pumps blood through the body, or to the seat of one's emotions. These definitions are not even similar, much less interchangeable.

Similarly, the proper translation of the Hebrew word "*goyim*" depends on the context—how it is used in the sentence. It is also important to consider how the human author of a biblical text would have understood his own words in the time period in which he spoke or wrote. In this case, it is unlikely that Jacob differentiated between Jews and non-Jews.

In his time, there was no such thing as a Jewish nation. Unlike a nation-state or other formal social group, the descendants of Jacob didn't use specific language to differentiate between insiders and outsiders; they were just a family, a "loosely organized kinship group," numbering about seventy. The word *goy*, as Jacob would have used it, meant nothing more than a people group or a tribe. [38]

Jacob's prophecy, then, in its plain sense, means simply that Ephraim's descendants would be great in number and would comprise many clans. This prophecy could have easily found its fulfillment in the prosperous Northern Kingdom of Israel; the tribe of Ephraim was so populous and influential there that its name eventually became synonymous with the Northern Kingdom itself.

This key passage, then, which supposedly helps root the Two-House movement in the formative years of Israel's history, is better understood as referring to the historical Jewish people. There is little reason to believe that the blessing of Ephraim was not both fulfilled by the people group known in the First Temple Period as "Israelites" and who are today known as the Jews.

One might ask: Is it not possible that there is a multifaceted meaning to the passage? Might the word *goyim* in Genesis 48:19 prophetically hint at the existence of Ephraimites among the nations? Doesn't Jewish tradition leave room for interpretations beyond the plain meaning of the text? The answer is yes, but it is illuminating to see how the New Testament authors themselves interpreted Old Testament prophecies that hinted at the phenomenon of Gentile association with Israel. While the New Testament evidence is discussed below, one example will suffice here: that of Genesis 17:4.

This passage records God's promise to Abraham that he will become the father of many nations (*hamon goyim*). Two-House teachers point to this passage as well, claiming that it finds its fulfillment in modern-day Christianity.[39] Here they are very close to Paul's own interpretation in Romans 4, which interprets the same promise to mean that many nations (i.e., not just Israel) would become Abraham's children through faith. Yet the focus of the Two-House movement is on biological ancestry, while Paul makes no such inference. For Paul, the conversion of Gentiles to Jewish monotheism constitutes the fulfillment of God's promise. This concept will be explored further in chapter four.

Yet it is important to note now that while Paul could have easily understood Genesis 17:4 literally and applied it to his Gentile converts, he did not. If Paul were a Two-House theologian, he could have taken the opportunity in Romans 4 to speculate on the supposed Israelite ancestry of his converts. Instead, he interprets Genesis 17:4 to mean that non-Israelites, Gentiles, would *become* Abraham's children by faith.

House of Israel, House of Judah

Another set of passages that undergird Two-House theology has to do with the perennial dichotomy between the Northern and Southern Kingdoms. Wootten claims that descendants of the ten tribes which populated the Northern Kingdom "were never once called 'Jews.'"[40] It follows that according to Wootten, all references to the Jews in the prophetic literature and the New Testament must refer only to the southern tribes. Wootten postulates that the division between the northern and southern tribes still exists and that they must still be understood as two separate and distinct entities.[41]

As discussed above, the kingdom was split in two after Solomon's reign; ten tribes were given to Jeroboam and two (or three, or perhaps even four)[42] to Rehoboam. Jeroboam's tribes constituted the Northern Kingdom; Rehoboam's constituted the Southern. First the Northern, then the Southern Kingdom descended into idolatry and was deported. As Two-House proponents claim, it is clear that the two kingdoms were separate entities. They are addressed separately in the books of the Kings and Chronicles, and the prophets address them separately as well.

Yet the border between the two kingdoms was porous. Even as early as the beginning of Rehoboam's reign, members of all the tribes migrated to the Southern Kingdom to worship God in Jerusalem, according to 2 Chronicles 11:16–17. Another migration occurred during the reign of King Asa, as recorded in 2 Chronicles 15:9. Again during the reign of Hezekiah, many from the North came down to Jerusalem to worship God, though they apparently returned to their ancestral lands afterward (2 Chronicles 30–31). Nevertheless, during these migrations, apparently many from the northern tribes permanently assimilated into the Southern Kingdom.

The deportation of the Northern Kingdom is recorded in 2 Kings 17: "In the ninth year of Hoshea, the king of Assyria captured Samaria, and he carried the Israelites away to Assyria and placed them in Halah, and on the Habor, the river of Gozan, and in the cities of the Medes." This event is also recorded in several inscriptions by the Assyrian king Sargon II, who claimed responsibility for the fall of Israel:

[The inhabitants of Sa]merina, who agreed [and plot-
ted] with a king [hostile to] me, not to endure servitude
and not to bring tribute to Assyria and who did battle, I
fought against them with the power of the great gods, my
lords. I counted as spoil 27,280 people, together with their
chariots, and gods, in which they trusted. I formed a unit
with 200 of [their] chariots for my royal force. I settled the
rest of them in the midst of Assyria.[43]

Scholars estimate that the population of the Northern Kingdom
before the deportation was around 400,000 people.[44] Even if many
more inhabitants of the Northern Kingdom were deported than are
recorded in Sargon's inscription, it seems likely that more remained
than were deported, and that the impact of the deportation was
largely psychological.[45]

David Baron further points out that "about a century after the
fall of Samaria, we find in the reign of Josiah some of Manasseh
and Ephraim 'and a remnant of all Israel' [2 Chronicles 34:9] in
the land, who contributed to the collection made by the Levites
for the repair of the house of the Lord in Jerusalem."[46] So not only
did many Israelites remain in the northern territories; they even
continued to have a relationship with the southern tribes.

This is not to argue that the biblical account of devastating
exile in 2 Kings and the prophetic literature is inaccurate. The
penalty of exile, including the loss of political sovereignty which
the Northern Kingdom incurred, was harsh, and the prophets
definitely perceived the northern tribes as being in exile, awaiting a
final ingathering, despite the fact that many remained in the land.
However, it is important to note that the Scripture does not lead
us to believe that the northern tribes were utterly destroyed as a
people or even that they were deported down to the last man. The
bulk of the ten northern tribes did assimilate—not into Assyria,
though, but rather into Judah.

By the time of Cyrus the Great, who allowed all Jews throughout
his kingdom to go back to their native land, the Assyrian Empire
had been swallowed up by the Babylonians, who in turn were
conquered by the Persians. Consequently, any Israelites from the
Northern Kingdom who had retained their identity through the
Assyrian exile would have been free to return to Israel under the

decree of Cyrus.[47] The Persians did not differentiate between tribal identities and referred to all Israelites as "Jews."[48] Jewish tradition agrees: "*Tosafos* to *Gittin* 36a concludes that during the period of the second Temple there were representatives of all twelve tribes in Israel."[49]

Many[50] of those who were deported from the Northern Kingdom did not return; those who lost their identity as Israelites would have assimilated into Assyrian society and culture.[51] Their descendants would be found today among the Syrian people, many of whom are Christian and belong to various Oriental churches (the Assyrian Church of the East and the Syriac Orthodox Church among others) which split off from Catholicism after the Council of Chalcedon in 451 CE. This is one case in which a non-Jewish people group might have some claim to significant Israelite ancestry. Yet one rarely (if ever) hears Two-House proponents single the Syrian people out as potential "Ephraimites."

The later prophetic literature seems to confirm that the two houses remained separate, with numerous parallel references to Israel and Judah. These passages appear to address or portray them as separate entities. The prophets repeatedly prophesy to both houses even after the deportation of both kingdoms. One passage in particular clearly speaks of their reunification as one indivisible body (Ezekiel 37:15–28), and it is a passage that, at least toward its end, is clearly referring to the Messianic Age. This seems to imply that the reunification of the people of Israel has not yet been accomplished and will not be until Messiah returns.

One critic of the Two-House movement has argued that these passages are not really referring to two separate entities. She notes that parallelism is a common rhetorical device in Hebrew, especially Hebrew poetry. Often the rhetorical point of placing two ideas, concepts, or words together in parallel is to equate them, not differentiate between them.[52] In other words, the fact that the prophets repeatedly address Israel and Judah together in parallel language is not, she argues, evidence that they are distinct or that the prophet must use both terms to include all of the children of Israel. Rather, it may be an indication that the prophet considers Judah and Israel to be synonymous terms.

This interpretation, though, falls short. The prophets continue to address Israel and Judah as separate nations even after their deportation and not only in poetic parallelisms. Both Israel and Judah are separately promised that they will return to their land. In the time of the later prophets, the separate socio-historical identities of the Northern and Southern kingdoms had been a concrete reality for centuries. To argue that they were suddenly equated on the basis of an argument from Hebrew poetry seems to ignore the historical context and the very real division between the two kingdoms. The prophets' poignant reminders that God would unite Israel and Judah make no sense if the two terms were already considered identical.

Among the prophetic passages which mention Israel and Judah as separate entities, the most striking is Ezekiel 37, a prophetic oracle which promises the reunification of both houses into one entity.[53] The fact that this event is connected with the ingathering of the exiles and the Messianic reign strongly implies that Ezekiel is referring to an end-time, apocalyptic scenario. The front cover of Batya Wootten's book *Who is Israel?* is a painting of the dramatic uniting of two sticks which God instructed Ezekiel to perform in front of the Judean exiles to signify their reunion with the dispersed tribes of the North, as recorded in Ezekiel 37. This passage is central to Two-House theology, which holds that the reunification of the tribes is yet in the future, and that at some point "Ephraimites" will join with the Jewish people in the land of Israel as one body. It seems to be assumed that if no descendants of the Northern Kingdom exist as a separate people, then they cannot reunify with the descendants of Judah, and the prophecy cannot be fulfilled.

Ezekiel's prophecy certainly has elements that are unfulfilled. However, there are numerous instances in the Prophets in which prophecies relating to the Messianic Age and prophecies relating to the lifetime of the prophet are placed together without distinction. One obvious example is Jeremiah 31:31–40. This prophecy is alluded to by Jesus at the Last Supper, when he indicated that he was in the process of inaugurating it. It is by the New Covenant that the believer's sins are forgiven, yet many of its other terms remain unfulfilled, such as the promise that no one will need to be taught about God.

Another familiar example is Isaiah 61, which Jesus begins to quote in Luke 4:16–20. Though Jesus announced that he had come to fulfill that prophecy, there are many elements of Isaiah's oracle that were not fulfilled by Jesus during his lifetime. Certainly Jesus proclaimed good news to the poor (v. 1), but he did not raise up the ancient cities (v. 4). Isaiah did not differentiate between those aspects of his prophecy which would be fulfilled by Jesus during the incarnation and those aspects which would have to wait until a later time. In retrospect, it is clear which parts of the oracle Jesus came to fulfill, but in Isaiah's day as well as in Jesus' day, it was not so clear.

Similarly, the different aspects of Ezekiel's prophecy need not be fulfilled at the same time or even close together in time. It is not beyond the realm of possibility that the reunification of the twelve tribes as one unit would happen in Ezekiel's lifetime (sixth century BCE) or shortly thereafter, and that the rest of the prophecy would be fulfilled centuries or even millennia later. In fact, one Two-House critic has argued just that, claiming that the return under Ezra constituted the awaited ingathering of the exiles.[54]

Nevertheless, it is obvious that, though there was a *partial* fulfillment in the days of the returning exiles under Ezra, and even in the migrations of many members of the Ten Tribes down to the Southern Kingdom in the days of the great kings of Judah, most Jews from all twelve tribes still remain in exile today. Ezekiel's prophecy that Israel and Judah would be reunited in the land under the Davidic Messiah is, as Two-House proponents claim, yet to be fulfilled.[55]

Yet the Jewish people comprise the only people group today that can claim an unbroken continuity with these historical Israelites. As discussed above, while some members of the Ten Tribes were lost to the Assyrian captivity, many more were assimilated into the Jewish people. So while in some sense the ten tribes could be described as "lost" because they no longer remember their tribal identity, their descendants today are mostly found within the Jewish people.

Even at that, there are, in fact, many descendants of the exiles from all twelve tribes to be found among the Gentiles. These people may have Jewish ancestry and not even know it. Yet this is no basis on which to form a theology of identity. The identification of these "lost" Jews is properly part of the ingathering of the exiles and the restoration of the Davidic kingdom, as the prophets Ezekiel and Hosea make clear. Two-House proponents—even those like J. K. McKee who refuse to identify themselves positively as physical Israelites[56]—argue that they should have a certain standing within the Jewish community based on prophecies regarding the ingathering of the exiles.[57] This eschatological event, though, is accomplished by the Messiah, not by a gut feeling that one is an Israelite, by fruitless speculation as to ancestry, or by claiming an identity that the apostles did not accord to non-Jewish believers.

David Baron sums up the attitude of the post-exilic prophets toward the two houses of Israel and Judah:

> The point, however, to be noticed in this and other prophecies is the clear announcement which they contained that the purpose of God in the schism—as a punishment on the House of David—was now at an end, and that henceforth there was but one common hope and one destiny for the whole Israel of the Twelve Tribes—whether they previously belonged to the northern kingdom of the Ten Tribes, or to the southern kingdom of the Two Tribes—and that this common hope and destiny was centered in Him Who is the Lion of the Tribe of Judah, and the rightful Heir and descendant of David.[58]

The New Testament Evidence

A survey of what the New Testament has to say about the two houses of Israel should either confirm or challenge the claims of Two-House theology. If Jesus and the apostles believed that their ministry involved re-gathering lost Israelites who had forgotten their identity, surely they would have mentioned it. However, a careful reading of the New Testament indicates rather clearly that neither Jesus nor the apostles identified Gentiles as Israelites who had lost their identity.

The apostles consistently divide humanity into two groups: on the one hand is Israel, also called the Jews; on the other hand are the Gentiles, also called Greeks.[59] These two categories are all-inclusive; the idea that there are assimilated, lost tribes of Israel waiting to rediscover their identity is nowhere hinted at in the text (though again, the identifiable Jewish Diaspora looms large). Nevertheless, a few passages that seem to hint at the ten lost tribes are emphasized by Two-House teachers.

One common example is Matthew 15:24, in which Jesus said, "I was sent only to the lost sheep of the house of Israel." To some Two-House teachers, this appears to be a reference to the ten lost tribes, who are supposedly dispersed throughout the Gentile nations.[60] However, according to the Gospel narratives, Jesus' ministry was conducted solely among the Jewish people, with very few exceptions.[61] In Matthew 10:5–6, Jesus explicitly contrasts the "lost sheep of the house of Israel" with the Gentiles: "These twelve Jesus sent out, instructing them, 'Go nowhere among the Gentiles and enter no town of the Samaritans, but go rather to the lost sheep of the house of Israel.'"[62] This terminology makes it very difficult to argue that what the Old Testament called the "House of Israel" (comprising the northern tribes) was not largely to be found *in Judea among the Jews* during the time of Christ.[63]

Revelation 21:12 is also cited by Two-House proponents to prove the idea that all of God's people must be Israelites. As New Jerusalem has only twelve gates, and they are named after the twelve tribes, it is thought that one must have to belong to one of the tribes to enter the city.[64] Yet this exegesis is unsupported by sound study. David Aune writes, "Certainly there is no thought that each gate is reserved for use only by members of the tribe after which it is named... The mention of the twelve tribes implies that the New Jerusalem is not simply a city but rather the focal point of the entire land."[65] Moreover, Robert Mounce notes that the gates of the city are said to be perpetually open, and members of the nations are specifically recorded as coming into the city in Revelation 21:24-27.[66]

The rest of the New Testament evidence also points in quite a different direction than that of Two-House theology. For example, when Cornelius, a Gentile, is filled with the Holy Spirit as recorded in Acts 10, the apostles are shocked. They are caught off guard. The Cornelius event completely blew away their expectations, and a council eventually had to be called to address the "Gentile problem." At this council, recorded in Acts 15, no one proposes that Cornelius may be a descendant of the ten lost tribes. Everyone at the council agrees that the Gentiles who are coming to faith are just that—Gentiles. What they disagree on is whether or not they should have to convert to Judaism through the ritual of circumcision.[67] Clearly, no one at the council thought that the Gentiles were latent Israelites waiting to discover their ancestry.

Another New Testament passage particularly pertinent to the subject is James 1:1. James addresses his letter to "the twelve tribes in the Dispersion." While New Testament scholars have classically appropriated the title "twelve tribes" for the church and therefore infer that James's epistle was written to believers, both Jew and Gentile,[68] more recent commentators like Scot McKnight understand James to be referring to Messianic Jews.[69]

Furthermore, James was conscious that some of his Jewish audience could trace their ancestry back to the Assyrian captivity. McKnight writes: "The expression 'twelve tribes' could be seen as almost *per definitionem* metaphorical: ten of those tribes have been lost since the Assyrian captivity. But it is not that easy. Jews with plausible connections back to the eighth-century deportation were present in the Diaspora in the first century, and the hope of their return was a routine feature of Jewish eschatology."[70]

Further fleshing out the state of the Diaspora in the first century, Richard Bauckham writes about the ten northern tribes:

> Descendants of those who had been deported by the Assyrians in the eighth century BCE were still living in the lands to which they had been deported—north Mesopotamia and Media—and formed an important part of the eastern Diaspora. In the first century CE contact between these people and Jerusalem was well maintained. They sent their temple tax to Jerusalem and came themselves on pilgrimage when possible. Rabbi Nahum the Mede—who must have originated from the Israelite communities in Media—was a well known Pharisaic leader in Jerusalem.[71]

All of this is not to say that Jesus and the apostles were not concerned about the Diaspora or the ingathering of the exiles. The great shofar which heralds the ingathering of the elect from the four winds (Matthew 24:31) and the sheep from a different pen that will be brought in to form one flock (John 10:16) are references to the Diaspora, including the scattered remnants of those descended from the northern exiles. As the prophesied Messiah, Jesus will bring together the Jewish people from wherever they have been scattered. Some Rabbinic traditions even postulate that Jews who have lost their Jewish identity will be included in this ingathering. Two-House teachers have particularly emphasized these traditions, which will be discussed below.

The Ten Tribes in Extra-Biblical Literature

A survey of the Old Testament evidence above led to the conclusion that although many from the Northern Kingdom migrated to Judah before the exile, and many who were exiled returned after the decree of Cyrus, there were some from the Northern Kingdom who remained in exile after the return of the Babylonian exiles to Judea. While the post-exilic literature appears to validate the idea that those exiles from all twelve tribes were still identifiable and were able to respond to the call for repentance and to return from exile, and while James expected his epistle to reach all twelve tribes, Two-House theology depends on the idea that the exiles from the northern tribes lost their identity and became Gentiles.[72] However, extra-biblical literature from the Second Temple period assumes that the ten tribes still exist in some identifiable form.

Josephus wrote in the first century CE, nearly 800 years after the Assyrian exile. One would expect that if the ten tribes had been truly lost, he would either mention that they had been lost or omit them from his history of the return of the exiles. However, Josephus wrote that "the ten tribes are beyond Euphrates till now [i.e., until the first century CE], and are an immense multitude, and not to be estimated by numbers."[73]

Another work from the same period, 4 Ezra, also mentions the ten tribes. According to this apocryphal work, the ten tribes "took this counsel among themselves, that they would leave the multitude of the heathen, and go forth into a further country, where never mankind dwelt, that they might there keep their statutes, which they never kept in their own land." The author of 4 Ezra goes on to document their miraculous passing through the Euphrates to a place called "Arsareth," from which they will not come back until "the latter time."[74]

Both of these works allege that the ten tribes *retained* their identity as Jews. Both of them place the ten tribes across the Euphrates River. Both of them were written nearly 800 years after the Assyrian captivity began. Like James, both Josephus and the author of 4 Ezra appear to have knowledge of (or assume the existence of) descendants of the ten tribes who still identify and practice as Jews, and who live in the same locations to which they were originally dispersed. Notably though, unlike James, Josephus and especially the author of 4 Ezra begin to ascribe legendary traits to these tribes. The miraculous and legendary manner of their exile and coming return in 4 Ezra constitutes the first identifiable hint of the ten lost tribes myth.[75]

Perhaps based on this sparse first-century account, later readers tried to identify the specific location of the Ten Tribes; one can conjecture that at some time it became clear that no people group matching the legend recorded in 4 Ezra still existed across the Euphrates.[76] The Talmud and Midrash place them across a miraculous river called the Sambatyon or the Sabbatyon, which stops flowing on the Sabbath; at Daphne at Antioch; and at an unknown location covered by a cloud.[77] David Baron notes that these legendary accounts are evidence of "how early people's minds became muddled on this subject."[78]

Now, for the other side of the coin: What about those from all twelve tribes, discussed above, who *have* assimilated into Gentile culture and lost their identity as Israelites? What does the extra-biblical literature say about them? Interestingly, Judaism has preserved a tradition that they will, as Two-House proponents claim, rediscover their identity. "Mashiach will even reveal that some of the 'gentiles' who brought the Jews to Yerushalayim are in reality Jews, who inadvertently became assimilated and don't even know of their Jewish origin! Such Jews will also be returned to the fold, and the [priests and Levites] among them will be reinstated in their proper positions."[79]

It is apparent, though, as we have argued, that the identification of these lost Jews does not happen until the Messiah comes and re-gathers the exiles. This event is identified by Jesus as part of the *parousia*, the Second Coming, in Matthew 24:31. To try to claim a status as an Israelite before the great shofar and the coming of Messiah is to construct a theology of identity on speculation, not fact. It may be true that Israelites walk among the nations, but it does not follow that Gentile believers in Jesus should claim that identity for themselves or associate themselves with prophecies about the re-gathering of the exiles of Israel (as against prophecies about Gentiles who attach themselves to Israel)—something the early Gentile believers appear never to have done.

Taken as a whole, the textual evidence from the books of Moses through the end of the first century does not support Two-House theology. The northern tribes did not all lose their identity as children of Israel and assimilate into Gentile society; instead, they mostly assimilated into Judah and continue to be part of the Jewish people today. While there are undoubtedly descendants of the assimilated portions of both Ephraim and Judah alive today, and there is reason to believe these exiles will rediscover their identity when Messiah comes, speculation that one may be descended from the exiles is no basis on which to form a theology of identity. Rather, non-Jewish believers should allow the Apostolic Writings—the New Testament—to form their identity, as will be discussed in chapter four.

We have finished surveying the textual evidence. However, there are other issues with Two-House theology that deserve consideration. Two-House theology is not merely unbiblical; it has severe ramifications for the church and for the Jewish people.

CHAPTER THREE

OTHER ISSUES WITH TWO-HOUSE THEOLOGY

Two-House theology, like any other theology, has ramifications that are not immediately obvious. Martin Luther's challenge to Catholicism was intended to reform a few practices that he considered unbiblical and immoral; the Reformation it sparked has had huge unintended cultural and religious consequences. To hit a bit closer to home, the apostolic fathers of the church probably had no idea that their theology of Jews and Judaism would eventually lead to mass persecution of Jews. The dehumanization of the Jews by the church in medieval Europe laid the foundation for secular anti-Semitism and, ultimately, the Holocaust.

Two-House theology also has consequences. Its view of the Jewish people is unsettling, and many of its advocates draw on philosophies and theories that are, at their core, racist and discriminatory. Also pertinent is the genetic evidence that has been unearthed since the formative years of Two-House theology. Like any claim to ancestry or genetic relationship, the claims of Two-House advocates can now be tested scientifically. The results are not favorable to the Two-House movement.

It's All in the Genes

Two-House theology is centered on the theory that some, many, or all modern Christians may be descendants of the ten lost tribes of Israel. If this claim is true, then modern Christians should have genetic markers that link them to the Jewish people. Two-House advocate Batya Wootten, however, believes that "genetic connection to the patriarchs absolutely cannot be proven;" she claims this is the case both for Jews and for non-Jews.[80] At best, this is an argument from ignorance; the fact that one cannot prove he is descended from Abraham does not mean that anyone can claim he is descended from Abraham. At worst, it is an attack on the legitimacy of the Jewish people.

Several important genetic studies have been done that shed doubt on Wootten's remarks. Oddly enough, one of them is found in a footnote to her statement quoted above. A 1997 study indicated that a large percentage of both Ashkenazi and Sephardic families with strong traditions of being *kohanim*—priests, descendants of Aaron—were probably descended from a single population in the Second Temple period.[81] The next year, another study revealed that these priestly families were, in all likelihood, descended from a single man who lived over 3,000 years ago.[82]

Later studies went further. By expanding the number of genetic markers being studied, as well as the sample sizes, it was determined that all Jewish people throughout the world had common genetic markers. These genetic markers set them apart from the Gentile populations that surrounded them. Even after centuries of accepting proselytes into their numbers, Jews from all the countries into which they have been dispersed have a genetic relationship to each other and to other people groups in the Levant.[83]

For those who do not accept the historical claim of the Jewish people to be a single ethnic group with its origins in the land of Israel, it must be astounding to see this claim verified by modern scientific studies. Certainly Wootten's contention that the Jewish people cannot prove that they are descendants of Abraham now falls short. The unbroken tradition of the Jewish people's ancestry is supported by the scientific evidence of recent genetic studies. Taken together, they provide convincing evidence that the Jewish people really are descendants of Abraham and that they did inhabit the land of Israel.

These same studies compared Jewish genes to the genes of other people groups. If one could see ethnic groups as clusters of people on a map, with their proximity to each other based on how closely they are related, one would see that the Jewish people form a coherent unit on the map, a unit that is far more closely related to modern-day Levantine populations than it is to the other major clusters such as Caucasians, Asians, and Africans. If Two-House claims were true, and large numbers of non-Jews in fact had significant Jewish ancestry, one would expect that these relationships would show up in genetic studies. But they do not.

What about assimilation, though? Certainly many Gentiles have Jews in their genealogy, Jews who have assimilated and intermarried with Gentiles. Yet while it is definitely true that Jews over the millennia have assimilated into Gentile culture, having a few Jewish ancestors does not make one Jewish. Rather, Jews must be circumcised according to Jewish tradition in order to retain their status as Jews. It was this very action—circumcision—that formed the basis for the dispute in Acts 15 about whether or not Gentile converts had to become Jewish. It follows that children of Jews who are not circumcised are not considered Jewish, regardless of their genetic ancestry.[84] To reenter Judaism, they must approach Judaism on Judaism's own terms and convert as proselytes.

Alternatively, it is absolutely possible that when Messiah returns, he will reveal the exiles who have been lost among the nations and bring them back into the fold of Israel. Such an event would certainly confirm Jewish eschatological expectations, as discussed above. Yet again, it must be stressed that this event is beyond the prophetic horizon. According to the New Testament and Jewish tradition, the ingathering of the exiles is accomplished by Messiah personally. Arguing for any particular congregational polity based on this unfulfilled prophecy runs against the teaching of the New Testament.

Two-House Theology and Latent Supersessionism

As discussed above, Two-House exegetes like Batya Wootten reject Jewish tradition. This includes Judaism's definition of who is and is not Jewish, among other Rabbinic traditions.[85] Throughout her book, Wootten transliterates the four-letter name of God; this is considered extremely offensive in Judaism, whose adherents hold that the name of God should not be pronounced except in certain (very narrow) circumstances.[86] Importantly, Wootten even questions whether or not Jews can prove they are descended from Abraham: "At this point in history, genetic connection to the patriarchs absolutely cannot be proven. This fact, of course, is true for Jew and non-Jew alike."[87] For a Jew, all of these rejections of Jewish tradition ring some serious alarm bells.

Since their exile in 135 CE, Jews have been without a homeland. Their traditions, rooted in the Mosaic Law, have preserved them as a distinct people group. It is obvious how some of these traditions, such as the prohibition of intermarriage and the definition of who is and is not Jewish, have helped to preserve the identity of the Jewish people. Furthermore, Jewish dietary laws, religious apparel, and distinctive customs have always identified the Jewish people as a distinct people group and prevented them from being completely assimilated into the cultures and peoples among whom they have been dispersed.

Any challenge to this identity is likely to be perceived, from a Jewish perspective, as an attack on the Jewish people themselves. It should not be hard to understand why. Unlike a conventional nation which has borders and laws connected to the land within those borders, Jews were without a homeland for over 1,800 years. Other nations have laws and borders, and police and armies to enforce them. Being part of the Jewish people is different; it is voluntary. The traditions which united the Jewish people were able to preserve them through the long Diaspora. These traditions which inform and protect Jewish identity are of the utmost value to the Jewish people.

Two-House theology, like traditional supersessionist Christian theology, makes no distinction between Jew and believing Gentile.[88] Instead of simply erasing the identity of the Jewish people in the body of Christ, as supersessionist theology does, Two-House theology claims that believing Gentiles are actually Israelites (a term that in Judaism is restricted to Jews). The effect, though, is the same: being Jewish doesn't matter anymore. It is not a special, unique, distinctive status, for it means nothing to be Jewish if anyone can make a legitimate claim to being Jewish. The net effect is that Jews are no longer considered a distinct people. In essence, Jews become extinct.[89]

The Jewish people are particularly sensitive to the ramifications of any theology that diminishes or erases Jewish identity. For over a thousand years, the church persecuted Jews and often forced them to convert to Christianity. These converted Jews were prohibited from observing the commandments of the Mosaic Law. They were disallowed from practicing their ancient customs. As a result, they lost their identity as Jews. Their children grew up as Gentiles.

If Two-House advocates were to approach the Jewish people on Jewish terms, they would find that they must undergo ritual proselytization in order to claim a Jewish (or "Israelite") status. This would be true even if there were some Jewish ancestry in their genealogy. Two-House proponents, though, largely reject Judaism and its traditions. They make a claim on the rights and responsibilities of the Jewish people without taking the steps to be recognized by the Jewish people as Jews.

As a consequence, the Two-House movement is likely to be interpreted by Jews as a direct attack on Jews and Judaism. Jack Carstens rightly states that Two-House claims constitute "a complete usurpation of the Jewish national character,"[90] a complaint that cannot be made of Christianity or of mainstream Messianic Judaism. While no Two-House exegete would claim to be supersessionist or to be replacing Israel, this is certainly what it looks like from a Jewish perspective.

The sense of legitimacy that Two-House theology grants its followers can easily translate into a sense of entitlement—entitlement to the name "Israel," entitlement to interpret the Mosaic Law independently of Jewish (and Christian) exegetical tradition, even entitlement to the Right of Return—and while Ephraimites believe they are practicing a biblically sanctioned religion in solidarity with the Jewish people, the fact that Jews do not accept their claims will almost inevitably result in a negative stance taken toward the Jewish people. This stance is already manifested in the deprecation of Judaism and Jewish tradition that is widespread in the Two-House movement.

When Martin Luther first attempted to reform Catholic theology and practice, he thought that the Jewish people would accept his new portrayal of the Christian religion. Consequently, he was initially warm toward the Jewish people, and in 1523 he wrote a tract, *That Jesus Christ was Born a Jew*, highlighting the Jewishness of Jesus. In this tract he was sympathetic to the plight of European Jews and lambasted other Christians for their harsh treatment of the Jews.

Time passed, however, and by the end of his life, Luther was frustrated that the Jews had rejected his brand of Christianity. In 1543 he wrote one of the most famous anti-Semitic works of all time, *On the Jews and Their Lies*, advocating extremely harsh treatment for the Jewish people because they had failed to accept his reformed Christianity. One wonders if the Two-House movement will go down the same track if their claim to be Israelites fails to gain acceptance in the Jewish community.[91] In fact many Two-House teachers already vilify even Messianic Jews for failing to respond positively to their claims.[92]

This is not to insinuate that Ephraimites are anti-Semites. Though anti-Semitism often appears in the unlikeliest of places, on the whole Ephraimites love the Jewish people, pray for their well-being, and believe themselves to be working in the best interests of the Jewish people. Yet because they have staked a claim, so to speak, in Jewish territory, claiming to be Israelites, and because the rejection of this claim by the Jewish people is monolithic, the unintended consequences of Two-House theology may easily grow to include an anti-Jewish stance.[93]

The British-Israel Connection

Investigate the Two-House movement for yourself, and it won't be long before you begin to encounter names like Steven M. Collins and Yair Davidiy. Collins is associated with the remnants of what was once known as the "Worldwide Church of God," a Sabbatarian Christian denomination established by Herbert Armstrong.

Remember "British Israelism" from chapter one? Armstrong believed in it. He taught that the Anglo-Saxons were descendants of the ten northern tribes.[94] Collins has written several books in the same vein,[95] and a large number of Two-House proponents reference Collins's work.[96]

Yair Davidiy is also a widely referenced advocate of British Israelism. Because he is an Orthodox Jew and references many rabbinic traditions to support the British Israel theory, he has added credibility in the eyes of many Two-House proponents. Yet the extensive use of false etymologies and other forms of pseudo-scholarship seriously discredits his work and that of Collins.[97]

It's not hard to understand why Two-House theology and British Israelism might be identified with each other. Both teach that the northern ten tribes of Israel were lost and assimilated into Gentile nations. Both try to identify the descendants of these tribes. Significant portions of the Two-House movement come to the same conclusion as British Israelism—that the Anglo-Saxon nations are descendants of the northern ten tribes.[98] The two movements are so close that numerous Two-House proponents themselves seem unable to tell the difference between British Israelism and their own theology, referencing British Israelism advocates as Two-House sources.

An early opponent of British Israelism was Hebrew Christian (in modern terms, Messianic Jew) David Baron. His criticism of the British Israelite movement rings as clear today as it did nearly a hundred years ago, and is equally applicable to the modern Two-House movement:

> It diverts man's attention from the one thing needful, and from the only means by which he can find acceptance with God. This it does by teaching that "a nation composed of millions of practical unbelievers in Christ, and ripe for apostasy, in virtue of a certain fanciful identity between the mixed race composing that nation and a people carried into captivity two thousand five hundred years ago, is in the enjoyment of God's special blessing and will enjoy it on the same grounds for ever, thus laying another foundation for acceptance with God beside that which He has laid, even Christ Jesus" ... It not only robs the Jewish nation, the true Israel, of many promises in relation to their future by applying them to the British race [or "Ephraimites" –ed.] in the present time, but it *diverts attention from them as the people in whom is bound up the purpose of God in relation to the nations*, and whose "receiving again" to the heart of God, after the long centuries of unbelief, will be as "life from the dead to the whole world."[99]

Two-House theology and British Israelism both take the focus off the redemptive work of Jesus, remove the unique calling of the

Jewish people, and diminish the prophetic destiny of the believing Gentile in favor of baseless speculation about ancestry. They are so closely related that one wonders if the Two-House movement ever would have formed, were it not for the precedent set by the many legends about the ten lost tribes and the existence of British Israelism.

CHAPTER FOUR

GENTILE IDENTITY
IN MESSIAH

We have shown that the Two-House movement originated as a reaction to Messianic Judaism's insistence on being a Jewish movement. While it is loosely based on Scriptural exegesis, it draws heavily from myths and legends about the ten lost tribes. These tribes were, in reality, mostly assimilated into the Jewish people, losing only their historic tribal identity, not their identity as children of Israel. Furthermore, descendants of those who were assimilated into the Assyrian people have no way of knowing whether or not they have Israelite ancestry. Most importantly, Two-House proponents claim a status as Israelites based on nothing more than speculation, rather than accepting their status as Gentiles and waiting for the Messiah to bring about the final ingathering of the exiles.

But if Two-House theology is incorrect, the question it was designed to answer still remains. This is the "Gentile Question" from chapter one: If the Jews are still God's chosen people, what about believing Gentiles? How can Gentiles benefit from the covenants God made with the Jewish people without becoming Jewish? More practically, how can Gentiles who are drawn to the Torah and the Jewish people become involved with Messianic Judaism?

Essentially, it boils down to this: If Israel is limited to the Jewish people, and Israel is the people of God, where do believing Gentiles find their identity?

The classical answer to this question in Christian theology has been the doctrine of supersessionism, defined by R. Kendall Soulen as "the traditional Christian belief that since Christ's coming the Church has taken the place of the Jewish people as God's chosen community, and that God's covenant with the Jews is now over and done."[100] This doctrine ties up all the loose ends; unfortunately, it leaves God's eternal covenant people out of the equation. Supersessionism looks like a great deal for the Christian Church, but it doesn't hold water when held up to the light of Scriptures like Romans 11 and Jeremiah 31.[101]

But when supersessionism is abandoned, the questions it sought to answer must be answered all over again. In this chapter, we propose to take a step forward toward a concrete theology of Gentile identity in Messiah. This theology has implications for Messianic Jewish/Christian relations, Gentile believers' obligations to God's commandments, and Christian ecclesiology.

The Good Centurion

The doctrine of supersessionism developed very early in Christian theology.[102] To form a theology of Gentile identity that does not depend on it requires understanding the early social, cultural, and religious situation of the earliest Gentile believers. We must experience the problem as it was first experienced. In other words, we must go back to the beginning.

As noted above, Jesus' ministry was not directed toward Gentiles. He had no Gentile disciples and rarely even encountered Gentiles. The "Gentile Problem" did not emerge until Acts 10 when a Gentile, Cornelius, was accepted by God and was imbued with the Spirit. The apostles considered this a *novum*, a new and unprecedented development.[103]

Cornelius, a Roman centurion and almost certainly an idolater involved in imperial cultic worship,[104] is nevertheless described by Luke as "a devout man who feared God with all his household, gave alms generously to the people, and prayed continually to God" (Acts 10:2). In the first century, many Gentiles attached themselves in some way to the Jewish community. These Gentiles were called "God-fearers."[105] Paula Fredricksen wrote that these Gentiles continued to worship the gods of the Roman Empire as well as—if they were not native Romans—their ancestral gods; to fail to do so would have angered the gods and resulted in severe punishment from civil authorities. Jews apparently had no problem accepting these pagan Gentiles into their midst as well as their financial contributions to the synagogue.[106]

Cornelius, then, had a secure identity as a pagan Roman centurion. He was an integral part of Roman culture and religion and even of the Roman military. Nevertheless, he prayed at the times of the Temple sacrifices.[107] He gave money to the Jewish community. He was held in high esteem by "the entire nation" (Acts 10:22). The life of a God-fearer might seem like somewhat of a contradiction, but it was the only option available for a Gentile who wanted to worship the God of Abraham outside of proselyte conversion, so Cornelius took it.

Everything changed on the day Cornelius, during his daily afternoon prayer, saw a vision of an angel. The angel told him, "Your prayers and your alms have ascended as a memorial before God. And now send men to Joppa and bring one Simon who is called Peter. He is lodging with one Simon, a tanner, whose house is by the sea" (Acts 10:4–6). This cryptic message left Cornelius in fear and wonder. He didn't even wait until the next morning to send men on their way to Joppa, which was over thirty miles away—more than a day's journey.

The next day, Peter had a vision of his own. He went up to pray on the roof of Simon the Tanner's house just as Cornelius's men were approaching the city. While he was praying, he got hungry, but before lunch was ready, he fell into a trance and saw "something like a great sheet" coming down from heaven with all kinds of animals on it—clean and unclean. A voice said, "Kill and eat!"

Peter wasn't *that* hungry. He told the voice, "No way! I've never eaten anything common or unclean!" These two words—*koinos* and *akathartos*, respectively, in the Greek—refer to food that is prohibited by Jewish law. *Koinos* (common) refers to prohibited mixtures, food sacrificed to idols, and other food that would normally be clean but which has become somehow contaminated. *Akathartos* refers to food that comes from an unclean animal, as defined by Leviticus 11.[108]

The voice's response was just as cryptic as the angel's message to Cornelius: "What God has made clean, do not call common." Unfortunately, this verse has been interpreted by many classical exegetes to mean that the food laws of the Torah had been abrogated. But Peter was an observant Jew; this interpretation evidently never entered his mind.[109] Instead, "Peter was inwardly perplexed as to what the vision that he had seen might mean" (v. 17).

Before he could think of anything, Cornelius's men arrived. The Holy Spirit ordered Peter to go with them, so he grabbed six of his friends and they set out the next morning. After a day and a half of travel they arrived in Caesarea. It had been four days since Cornelius's vision. Cornelius and his whole family were already gathered together to welcome Peter into their household. Cornelius, not knowing what else to do, told Peter the story of his vision and why he had called Peter there, and then asked Peter to fill in the blanks and explain what God was up to.

In one moment, it all became clear to Peter. The unclean animals on the sheet in his vision represented Gentiles. Cornelius had been accepted by God. The word he was supposed to give to Cornelius was the gospel: the story of Jesus' life, death, and resurrection, and the implications of these events for the Jewish people—and now, Peter realized, for the entire world. So Peter gave the message of the gospel to Cornelius and his family.

Then something happened that apparently took everyone by surprise. Cornelius and his family received an outpouring of the Holy Spirit and began "speaking in tongues and extolling God" (Acts 10:46). Seeing this, Peter commanded them to be baptized. They were, for all intents and purposes … well, the text doesn't tell us what they were. Until very recently, Cornelius had been a pagan Roman centurion. But what was he now?

When Peter took this news back to the other believers in Jerusalem, they were initially skeptical. But Peter told his story, backed up by his six friends who had witnessed the whole thing, and claimed that "God gave the same gift to them [Cornelius's family] as he gave to us when we believed in the Lord Jesus Christ." The Jerusalem church responded by glorifying God and saying, "Then to the Gentiles also God has granted repentance that leads to life" (Acts 11:18).

Being caught up in the fresh wind of God's activity among the Gentiles, none of the apostles or the other Jewish believers immediately attempted to formulate a theology of Gentile identity. They just rejoiced. As we seek to formulate—or perhaps more accurately, to rediscover—that same theology today, we must remember to keep our priorities straight. We must praise God that his activity is universal and that he gives the same Holy Spirit to all who believe.

But our questions still haven't been answered, and neither had the questions of the believing Jews in Jerusalem. Before too long, two elements emerged. One group, mostly Pharisees who had accepted Christ, did not recognize the eschatological significance of the miraculous conversion of Cornelius. They argued that these Gentile believers must become proselytes; they must convert to Judaism.

Others, though, dissented. One of them was Sha'ul, also known as Paul, who had just come back from a mission trip to Asia Minor (known today as Turkey). He, like Peter, had witnessed God working in the lives of Gentiles. He reported that many Gentiles had come to faith in Jesus. We know from Paul's epistles that he immediately forbade these Gentile converts from worshipping idols.[110] They could no longer be identified as pagans. So how were they to be identified?

While the "circumcision faction"—probably a majority—answered this question by requiring conversion to Judaism, Paul refused this answer to the Gentile problem. This conflict was resolved in Acts 15 at what is now called the Jerusalem Council. First, Paul's opponents made their case. Then Peter got up and told his story. Then Paul and Barnabas told theirs. They didn't give a theological reason for their position. They just told their stories.[111] For them, that was enough. They had seen firsthand how God had miraculously changed the hearts of the Gentiles who had attached themselves to Jesus. It was clear enough to Peter, Paul, and Barnabas that the Gentiles didn't need another status change. They had been accepted just as they were.

It was James, Jesus' brother, who gave a theological voice to the position of Peter and Paul. He quoted Amos 9:11–12: "'After this I will return and rebuild David's fallen tent. Its ruins I will rebuild, and I will restore it, that the rest of mankind may seek the Lord, even all the Gentiles who bear my name,' says the Lord, who does these things, things known from long ago." James reasoned that the wave of Gentiles who were coming to faith were a fulfillment of biblical prophecy. At this juncture, with James's ruling, it became *halachah*—law—within the early church that Gentiles did not have to become Jews. Not only that, but their identity was just as valid and as valuable as that of the Jews. They too had an eschatological significance, they too were a fulfillment of prophecy, and they too were called by God to be part of the body of believers, just as the Jews were.

At the Jerusalem Council, then, one aspect of the identity of the Gentile believers had been confirmed. They weren't Jews, and since the term "Jew" and "Israelite" had been synonymous since the Captivity,[112] they couldn't be called "Israelites" either.[113] They were still Gentiles.[114] But in the first century, the terms "Gentile" and "pagan" were synonymous.[115]

Knowing this, many Two-House proponents are offended at being called "Gentiles." To them, the terms "Gentile" and "pagan" are still synonymous today. They believe that Israel constitutes the only people of God. The negative connotation of the word *goy* in rabbinic literature only serves to confirm this sentiment. Yet the New Testament is clear that believing Gentiles are still called Gentiles. They remained members of the *ethnē*, the nations, and the apostles addressed them as such.[116]

Yet non-idol-worshipping Gentiles were virtually unheard of. There was no precedent. New words and concepts had to be created to explain this new phenomenon, or else familiar concepts had to be adapted. The latter route is the one the New Testament authors took in identifying the Gentile converts, their place in God's plan, and their obligations to God and to the Jewish people.

Metaphors for Gentile Conversion in Paul's Epistles

The task for defining the identity of Gentile converts was largely left to the Apostle Paul, the self-described "apostle to the Gentiles."[117] Modern social-scientific studies on the Bible have called Paul an "entrepreneur of identity"[118] or a "social entrepreneur"[119] who was engaged in forming the identity of his Gentile converts, creating for them a definition of who they were and mapping their relationships with other social groups.[120] To do this, Paul used some metaphors that were drawn from the Old Testament and others that were drawn from Roman society.[121] Taken together, they help give substance and definition to the identity of Gentile believers in Jesus. We will find that even though they do not become Jewish, neither do they remain an undifferentiated part of their pagan society.[122] Paul "invents" a new identity for them and uses variegated imagery to describe that identity.[123]

Romans 4:16–17 and Galatians 3:7–9 contain one of Paul's most powerful metaphors for describing Gentile identity. Paul claims that believing Gentiles are children of the forefather of the Jewish people, Abraham himself! His argument is that since Abraham believed when he was uncircumcised, he is not only the father of the Jews, his biological descendants, but also of all those throughout history who have had "the faith of Abraham."

It is worthwhile to note that Paul leaves out the other two forefathers of the Jewish people, Isaac and Jacob. By limiting Gentile identity to children of Abraham, he makes it clear that these Gentiles are not part of "Israel"—a name reserved for Jacob's descendants. However, God promised that Abraham would become the father of many nations, as recorded in Genesis 17:4. Paul sees the believing Gentiles as a fulfillment of that promise.[124] They are still members of the "nations" (Gr. *ethnē*, Heb. *goyim*) but their new identity allows them to be simultaneously children of Abraham (and therefore heirs to the promise of Abraham) and members of the nations.

Paul takes great pains to emphasize that the covenant of promise which helps define Gentile identity in Christ is the Abrahamic covenant and not the Sinai covenant. His repeated contrast of these two covenants, especially in Galatians, is meant to drive home the point that though the Gentile converts are children of Abraham, they are not children of Israel, nor did they stand at the foot of Mount Sinai and receive the Torah.[125] Despite their shared ancestry in Abraham and their shared inheritance in the promise to Abraham, believing Gentiles and Jews have differing obligations to God.[126]

Paul also includes his Gentile converts as citizens of a kingdom. Variously described as the "kingdom of God" (1 Corinthians 6:9–10; Galatians 5:19–21), the "kingdom of light" (Colossians 1:12), and the "kingdom of the Son" (Colossians 1:13), Paul uses "kingdom" to indicate the Gentile believer's eschatological political situation. In other words, who is the Gentile believer's ultimate authority? Is he still nothing more than a subject of the Roman emperor, while the Jewish people have an eschatological King to look forward to?

Paul's answer is that Gentile believers, like their Jewish brethren, are included in the reign of Jesus Christ. He is their King, and they are his citizens. They have transferred their allegiance from the reign of Caesar to the reign of Christ, a reign that will come into its fullness at his return. This metaphor may underlie the language of citizenship in a commonwealth in Ephesians 2, discussed below.

Paul used the imagery of slavery and freedom as well. He regarded Gentile idolaters as "slaves to sin" (Romans 6:20–21) and to "the weak and worthless elementary principles of the world" (Galatians 4:9). Typical of Jewish attitudes toward idolatry, Paul associated it with all kinds of immoral behavior—behavior that led naturally from idolatry, and that was in some way an involuntary consequence of idolatry, dictated by God (Romans 1:18–32).

This status of slavery has been removed through obedience to Christ (Romans 6:17–18). The Gentile believers are now free from sin and slaves to obedience (v. 16), to righteousness (v. 19), and to God (v. 22). Paul describes this process as redemption (*apolytrosis*), a word normally used to describe the ransom, or buying back, of prisoners of war or captive slaves.[127] Paul envisions his Gentile converts as more than just freed slaves; they are adopted children, brought into God's family (Galatians 4:5).

Another metaphor Paul uses is the term "in Christ" (Romans 8:1; 1 Corinthians 1:30; 2 Corinthians 5:17). In contrast to those who are "in Adam" (1 Corinthians 15:22), those who are in Christ "belong to the new aeon with its freedom and life."[128] Gentile believers are no longer identified with the old way of life that characterizes sinful humanity; "in Christ" they participate in the eschatological community that Christ inaugurated, the community that foreshadows the ultimate redemptive era, the World to Come.

"Salvation" or the idea of being "saved" is very common in the Pauline corpus and is probably the most popular term used today to describe the action that brings someone into the community of faith—and rightly so. Believers are saved, or rescued, from this world, just as the Jewish people were saved from slavery in Egypt or the captivity in Babylon.[129]

The Commonwealth of Israel

This has been by no means a complete list. Paul uses many other metaphors to describe the Gentile believer's new standing: reconciliation, justification, waking up, being sealed, and even receiving an invitation.[130] But in the midst of all these carefully chosen figures of speech, Paul never once calls his Gentile converts Jews, Israel, or Israelites.[131] The closest he gets is Ephesians 2:12–13, 19: "Remember that you were at that time separated from Christ, alienated from the commonwealth of Israel and strangers to the covenants of promise, having no hope and without God in the world. But now in Christ Jesus you who once were far off have been brought near by the blood of Christ … So then you are no longer strangers and aliens, but you are fellow citizens with the saints and members of the household of God."

One can see how this passage could be interpreted to say that formerly Gentile converts are now citizens of Israel and thereby Israelites. However, Ephesians scholar Andrew Lincoln argues that the terminology Paul uses (*politeia*, *sympolitai*) does not necessarily mean "right of citizenship," though it can have this meaning. In this passage, it more likely refers to a "constitutive government, state, or commonwealth."[132]

In other words, Paul is not necessarily arguing that Gentile converts are citizens of Israel; rather, taken together, these Gentile converts and the Jewish people constitute the "commonwealth of Israel," which David Rudolph describes as "a multinational expansion of Israel proper that has emerged in the form of the Church."[133] It must be further noted that these Gentile converts are called "heirs together with Israel" in Ephesians 3:6, again implying that they do not take on the identity of "Israel."

To reiterate, had Paul desired to make his readers believe they were part of Israel, or Israelites, he would have surely made it clear. However, the one time he comes close to teaching this in Ephesians 2–3, he uses distancing language—"commonwealth of Israel" rather than "Israel"; "together with Israel" rather than "as a part of Israel." It must be remembered that Paul is a "social entrepreneur" or an "entrepreneur of identity" who is attempting to form the identity of Gentile believers;[134] the social entity he is helping to create is new, and although Paul draws on Old Testament imagery to help define this entity, it is nonetheless different from the socio-historical people called "Israel."

Post-Supersessionist Theology and Gentile Identity

Supersessionism was an unfortunate development in the early church, and because of the intertwining threads of anti-Judaism, supersessionism, and the search for Gentile identity in the early church, the theology of Gentile identity was formed in concert with a triumphalist, supersessionist attitude toward the Jewish people. This theology, though, wasn't *completely* wrong. At its core, it was formed using biblical language. Christians are indeed adopted children; they participate in Christ; they are freed from sin; they are children of Abraham; they are saved; they are part of the commonwealth of Israel. When supersessionism is excised, the ecclesiology of the church changes, but there is no need to excise what is good in Christian theology. In large part, what the church has been teaching about Christians and their status before God for the past two thousand years has been correct and has been informed by the Scripture.

Forming a post-supersessionist ecclesiology which completely defines the identity of Gentile believers and their relationship to the Jewish people would be a monumental task, beyond the scope of this introductory work. We hope merely to show that the apostles confronted the same questions we confront today, and their answers to these questions must inform and guide our search for a concrete theology of Gentile identity in Christ. The metaphors and terminology used by the apostles, and not the speculative identity claims of the Two-House movement, must form the foundation of this theology of identity.

Most of all, the eschatological significance of the emergence of a group of non-idolatrous Gentiles who worship the God of Israel and attach themselves to the Messiah cannot possibly be overestimated. The apostles clearly perceived this nascent group of Christ-believing Gentiles as a fulfillment of Biblical prophecy, as proof of Jesus' Messiahship, and as evidence that the eschaton was imminent. The role of Gentile believers was pivotal in the early church *because they were Gentiles*, not because they were Israelites who had lost their identity.

CONCLUSION

O ur search has come to an end. We have found that the adopted son, who spent so many years looking for his biological parents and the fortune that he was supposed to inherit, belonged after all with his adopted family, and will receive his fortune through them. The ancestry of most non-Jews isn't prestigious or enviable. The only claim they can make is that through Jesus Christ they have eternal life and a relationship with God and with the historic people of God, the people of Israel.

But this claim is priceless. It is greater than any claim to ancestry. Paul had much to brag about in his pedigree, yet though he valued his Jewish identity, it was, relative to his inheritance in Christ, relatively insignificant.[135] How much more is the ancestry of modern-day Christians insignificant in light of the riches and glory of their adopted family—the family of Christ.

The apostles were shocked by the conversion of Cornelius. It is easy today to read the Cornelius-event as inevitable, as a natural consequence of Jesus' ministry. Christian theologians have been emphasizing the universality of the gospel message for so long that they, for the most part, have historically forgotten its particular focus on the redemption of Israel. But for the apostles, a non-pagan Gentile was a walking miracle.

Today, as we see the phenomenon of non-pagan Gentiles, of children of Abraham who are still members of the nations of the world yet have turned from sin and toward righteousness, let us see it as the apostles did. It is a miraculous sign of the imminent eschatological restoration of all things. Each non-Jew who comes to faith as Cornelius did brings the world one step closer to its final redemption. It brings the World to Come imperceptibly nearer.

It is tempting to look beyond the biblical text for solutions to legendary problems like the apparent disappearance of the ten lost tribes from the biblical record. But this removes the focus of our attention from what it should be: the miraculous work of Jesus Christ in turning the formerly pagan Gentiles into followers of God, citizens of the kingdom of heaven, and children of Abraham. This is the miracle that began with Cornelius, and it should inspire us with awe and reverence for God, just as it did the early church.

The modern-day rediscovery of the Hebrew roots of the Christian faith is an equally miraculous event. It is a reaffirmation of the calling and election of Israel. It has the potential to build bridges between Christians and the Jewish people, estranged for so long yet sharing an eschatological destiny as people of God.

The prophets of Israel recognized that when the Gentiles began to attach themselves to Israel and to Israel's God, not as members of Israel or usurpers of Israel's destiny but as sympathetic worshippers of the God of Abraham, it was a sign of the coming redemption (Zechariah 8). It was a boon for the Jewish people. Paul understood that if he was successful in his ministry to the Gentiles, it would cause the Jews to see his ministry in this light, and they would, as a result, accept Jesus as the Messiah of Israel and initiate the resurrection from the dead (Romans 11:12, 15). Paul could taste the closeness, the imminence of this event even in his day; how much more should it ignite our hearts with passion today!

Messianic Jews and Christians who are sensitive to their Jewish roots stand at two ends of a great bridge across which Christians receive the greatness of the Torah and the centrality of the Jewish people in God's redemptive plan, and across which the Jewish people can see, for the first time in untold centuries, Jesus as a legitimate Messianic candidate. When everyone on both sides of the bridge understands their role and the eschatological significance of their very existence, this interchange can benefit everyone.

But when some decide that they don't belong on their side of the bridge, that they are entitled to a position on the other side, it causes problems. When non-Jews pretend to be Jewish or claim to have a share in Israel's portion, or when Christians influence Jews to become estranged from their heritage, it causes the bridge to weaken and collapse. The vital connection between Christians and the Jewish people fails to be established.

In this light, the Two-House movement emerges as a distraction, and a dangerous one. The problem is not just that it is based on speculation regarding ancestry. It also takes its followers' focus off the redemption of the world through Jesus Christ and the role of both Jew and Gentile in God's redemptive plan. It blurs the distinction between Jew and Gentile. It encourages a sense of entitlement rather than a sense of humility and acknowledgement of the unique status of the Jewish people. It sets up a roadblock in the bridge of Jewish-Christian relations.

If you are a Gentile who believes in Jesus Christ, realize that your eschatological significance is just as great as that of the Jewish people. You are a fulfillment of ancient prophecy. You have a great calling, a high and noble calling that only a Gentile believer in Messiah can fulfill. Don't be ashamed of this identity or this calling; rather, embrace it and let it define you. Be as excited about the phenomenon of the believing Gentile as the Apostle Paul was. Starting on the Damascus road, Paul fought for his whole life to keep Gentiles from losing their identity as Gentiles within Judaism.

Furthermore, support the Messianic Jewish movement for what it is—Jesus-believing Jews who wish to keep the commandments and customs of the Jewish people, and Gentiles who have come alongside them in solidarity. But at the same time, know that as a Gentile you are not limited in the number of commandments you can take on. While your ancestors did not stand at the feet of Mount Sinai, your attachment through Messiah to the Land, the Scriptures, and the People of Israel may well manifest itself in the form of practices like keeping the Sabbath, keeping the dietary laws, and other marks of Torah, in solidarity with (not in replacement of) the Jewish people.

Our intention in reaffirming the difference between Jew and Gentile is not to limit Gentile involvement in Messianic Judaism or to quench anyone's desire to keep the commandments of the Torah; in fact, Toby Janicki has made a strong case that Gentile believers are obligated to the vast majority of the Torah's commandments in some way or another, and are welcome to observe the rest as well.[136] Rather than pour water on the fires of zeal for the Torah, our desire is only to keep our theology biblical, to distinguish as the

Scripture does between Jew and Gentile, and to reaffirm the amazing, unique, prophetic destiny of both in God's redemptive plan.

In the Messianic Era, all flesh will come to Jerusalem to worship the God of Israel there. Every secret thing will be revealed and every heart will be laid bare before God. Be found then in Jesus our Messiah, and let your actions in this unprecedented time reflect your status as a child of Abraham and a citizen of God's kingdom. Do not seek a status that is not yours, but rather, glorify God that he made you the person you are. Work within the calling to which God has called you, and in doing so, you will hasten the return of Messiah and the redemption of all things.

The day is coming when the holy city, the New Jerusalem, will descend, prepared as a bride adorned for her husband. The twelve gates of the city will be open, day and night. Three look to the east. Three to the north. Three to the south. Three to the west. Each gate is made of precious stone. The names of the twelve tribes of the sons of Israel are inscribed upon the gates, just as they were inscribed on the twelve stones of the high priest's breast piece.

Through which gate will you enter?

The Bible teaches that in Jesus, "the Gentiles are fellow heirs, members of the same body" with the Jewish people (Ephesians 3:6), and "fellow heirs with Christ" Himself (Romans 8:17). The point of the vision of the New Jerusalem is not to exclude the non-Jews from the city; rather the gates of Israel stand open to the Gentiles, beckoning them to enter into the eternal reward that God has prepared for His people. The vision of New Jerusalem is not one of exclusion but inclusion, as it says, "the kings of the earth will bring their glory into it, and its gates will never be shut by day … They will bring into it the glory and the honor of the Gentiles."

If I were a Gentile Christian and someone asked me, "What gate will you enter?", I would reply, "I will enter through the gate of Judah. Although I am not from that tribe, my Master is the son of David from the house of Judah." Shouldn't the king's bride pass through the king's gate? Shouldn't a man's servant enter through the same gate as his master?

Don't rely on your identity according to the flesh. Even if you were truly a descendant of the noble tribe of Naphtali or the ancient tribe of Zebulun, that identity would not guarantee entrance through either one of those gates: "For not all who are descended from Israel belong to Israel" (Romans 9:6). Instead, rely upon your identity in Jesus, born again as a child of God, a new creation, a fellow-heir with Christ himself in the house of God, a citizen of New Jerusalem.

Our Lord is coming; indeed, he is coming soon!

BIBLIOGRAPHY

Armstrong, Herbert W. *The United States and Britain in Prophecy*. Published without copyright, 1945.

Atzmon, Gil, Li Hao, Itsik Pe'er, Christopher Velez, Alexander Pearlman, Pier Francesco Palamara, Bernice Morrow, Eitan Friedman, Carole Oddoux, Edward Burns, and Harry Ostrer. "Abraham's Children in the Genome Era: Major Jewish Diaspora Populations Comprise Distinct Genetic Clusters with Shared Middle Eastern Ancestry." *American Journal of Human Genetics* 86 no. 6 (2010): 850–59.

Aune, David. *Revelation 17-22*. Word Biblical Commentary 52c. Nashville: Thomas Nelson, 1998.

Baron, David. *History of the Ten Lost Tribes: Anglo-Israelism Examined.* London: Morgan and Scott, 1915.

Bauckham, Richard. *James*. New Testament Readings. New York: Routledge, 1999.

Bauckham, Richard. *Gospel Women: Studies of the Named Women in the Gospels.* Grand Rapids: Eerdmans, 2002.

Behar, Doron, Bayazit Yunusbayev, Mait Metspalu, Ene Metspalu, Saharon Rosset, Jüri Parik, Siiri Rootsi, Gyaneshwer Chaubey, Ildus Kutuev, Guennady Yudkovsky, Elza K. Khusnutdinova, Oleg Balanovsky, Ornella Semino, Luisa Pereira, David Comas, David Gurwitz, Batsheva Bonne-Tamir, Tudor Parfitt, Michael F. Hammer, Karl Skorecki, and Richard Villems. "The Genome-Wide Structure of the Jewish People." *Nature* 466 no. 7303 (2010): 238–42.

Benite, Zvi Ben-Dor. *The Ten Lost Tribes: A World History*. Oxford: Oxford University Press, 2009.

Bloomfield, Sandy. "The Errors of 'The Ephraimite Error.'" Lebanon, TX: Messianic Israel Alliance, 2008.

Bockmuehl, Markus. *Jewish Law in Gentile Churches*. Edinburgh: T&T Clark, 2000.

Broshi, Magen and Israel Finkelstein. "The Population of Palestine in Iron Age II." *Bulletin of the American Schools of Oriental Research* 287 (1992): 47–60.

Brueggemann, Walter. *A Commentary on Jeremiah: Exile and Homecoming*. Grand Rapids: Eerdmans, 1998.

Byrne, Brendan. *Romans*. Sacra Pagina 6. Collegeville, MN: Liturgical Press, 1996.

Carstens, Jack. *Is the Church Ephraim?* 2d ed. Self-published in 2007.

Charlesworth, James H., ed., *The Old Testament Pseudepigrapha*, vol. 1: *Apocalyptic Literature and Testaments*. New York: Doubleday, 1983.

Cohn-Sherbok, Dan. *Messianic Judaism*. New York: Continuum, 2001.

Colijn, Brenda. *Images of Salvation in the New Testament*. Downers Grove, IL: IVP Academic, 2010.

Collins, Steven M. *The "Lost" Ten Tribes of Israel ... Found!* Boring, OR: CPA Books, 1995.

Davidiy, Yair. *Joseph: The Israelite Destiny of America*. Jerusalem: Brit-Am, 2001; repr. Russell-Davis, 2005.

Davids, Peter. *The Epistle of James*. New International Greek Testament Commentary. Grand Rapids: Eerdmans, 1982.

DeVries, Simon J. *1 Kings*. Word Biblical Commentary 12. Waco, TX: WORD, 1985.

Dunn, James. *The Theology of Paul the Apostle*. Grand Rapids: Eerdmans, 1998.

Eby, Aaron and Toby Janicki. *Hallowed Be Your Name*. Marshfield, MO: First Fruits of Zion, 2008.

Eby, Aaron. *Biblically Kosher.* Marshfield, MO: First Fruits of Zion, 2012.

Eisemann, Moshe. *Yechezkel: A New Translation with a Commentary Anthologized from Talmudic, Midrashic, and Rabbinic Sources.* Brooklyn: Mesorah, 2009.

Esler, Philip. *Conflict and Identity in Romans.* Minneapolis: Fortress, 2003.

Fredricksen, Paula. *Augustine and the Jews.* New York: Doubleday, 2008.

Fung, Ronald. *The Epistle to the Galatians.* New International Commentary on the New Testament. Grand Rapids: Eerdmans, 1988.

Howell, Justin. "The Imperial Authority and Benefaction of Centurions and Acts 10.34–43." *JSNT* 31 no. 1 (2008): 25–51.

Janicki, Toby. "What Is a Gentile?" *Messiah Journal* 101 (Summer 2009): 38–45.

Janicki, Toby. "We Are the God-Fearers." *Messiah Journal* 103 (Spring 2010): 33–38.

Janicki, Toby. "One Law for All." *Messiah Journal* 105 (Fall 2010): 24–31.

Janicki, Toby. *Tefillin.* Marshfield, MO: First Fruits of Zion, 2011.

Janicki, Toby. "The Gentile Believer's Obligation to the Torah of Moses." *Messiah Journal* 109 (Winter 2012): 45–62.

Kessler, Edward and Neil Wenborn. *A Dictionary of Jewish-Christian Relations.* Cambridge: Cambridge University Press, 2005.

Kinzer, Mark. "Messianic Judaism and Jewish Tradition in the 21st Century: A Biblical Defense of 'Oral Torah.'" Paper presented at the annual meeting of the Hashivenu conference, Pasadena, CA, 2003. Cited 14 February 2012. Online: http://www.hashivenu.org/index.php?option=com_docman&task=doc_download&gid=39&Itemid=268.

Kinzer, Mark. *Postmissionary Messianic Judaism: Redefining Christian Engagement with the Jewish People*. Grand Rapids, MI: Brazos, 2005.

Ladd, George Eldon. *A Theology of the New Testament*. Grand Rapids, MI: Eerdmans, 1993.

Lancaster, D. Thomas. "Lunar Calendar and Aviv Barley." Cited 14 February 2012. Online: http://ffoz.org/_php/download.php?file=Lunar-Calendar-and-Aviv-Barley.pdf.

Lancaster, D. Thomas. *The Holy Epistle to the Galatians*. Marshfield, MO: FFOZ, 2011.

Lincoln, Andrew. *Ephesians*. Word Biblical Commentary 42. Waco, TX: Word Books, 1990.

McKee, J. K. "'The Ephraimite Error': Critical Errors." Cited 14 February 2012. Online: http://tnnonline.net/israel/ee-ce/index.html.

McKee, J. K. "Cross-Examining the Two-House Teaching." Cited 14 February 2012. Online: http://tnnonline.net/israel/cross-examining-2house/index.html.

McKee, J. K. "One Law for All." Cited 14 February 2012. Online: http://tnnonline.net/torah/one-law/index.html.

McKee, J. K. "A Place Where Everyone Can Belong." Cited 14 February 2012. Online: http://tnnonline.net/messianic-issues/everyone-belong/index.html.

McKee, J. K. "Anti-Semitism in the Two-House Movement." Cited 14 February 2012. Online: http://tnnonline.net/israel/anti-semitism-2house/index.html.

McKnight, Scot. *The Letter of James*. New International Commentary on the New Testament. Grand Rapids: Eerdmans, 2011.

Michael, Boaz. *Encounters with an Ephraimite*. Unpublished white paper, 2003.

Michael, Boaz and D. Thomas Lancaster. "One Law and the Messianic Gentile." *Messiah Journal* 101 (Spring 2009), 46-70.

Moo, Douglas. *The Epistle to the Romans*. New International Commentary on the New Testament. Grand Rapids: Eerdmans, 1996.

Moo, Douglas. *The Letter of James*. Pillar New Testament Commentary. Grand Rapids: Eerdmans, 2000.

Mounce, Robert H. *The Book of Revelation*. New International Commentary on the New Testament. Grand Rapids: Eerdmans, 1998.

Nanos, Mark. *The Mystery of Romans: The Jewish Context of Paul's Letter*. Minneapolis: Fortress, 1996.

Nanos, Mark. *The Irony of Galatians: Paul's Letter in First-Century Context*. Minneapolis: Fortress, 2002.

Parfitt, Tudor. *The Lost Tribes of Israel: The History of a Myth*. London: Phoenix, 2002.

Rudolph, David. "Paul's 'Rule in All the Churches' (1 Cor 7:17–24) and Torah-Defined Ecclesiological Variegation." Paper presented at the American Academy of Religion (AAR) Conference, Christian Systematic Theology Section, Chicago, November 2, 2008.

Rudolph, David. "The Relationship between the Church and Israel." *Verge* 2 no. 2 (2010): 4.

Rudolph, David. *A Jew to the Jews: Jewish Contours of Pauline Flexibility in 1 Cor. 9:19–23*. Tübingen: Mohr Siebeck, 2011.

Sadan, Tsvi. "Halachic Authority in the Life of the Messianic Community." *Messiah Journal* 109 (Winter 2012): 13–26.

Shkul, Minna. *Reading Ephesians: Exploring Social Entrepreneurship in the Text*. New York: T&T Clark, 2010.

Silberling, Kay. "The Ephraimite Error." Position paper submitted to the International Messianic Jewish Alliance, 1999.

Skorecki, Karl, Sara Selig, Shraga Blazer, Robert Bradman, Neil Bradman, P. J. Waburton, Monica Ismajlowicz and Michael F. Hammer. "Y Chromosomes of Jewish Priests." *Nature* 385 no. 6611 (1997): 32.

Soulen, R. Kendall. *The God of Israel and Christian Theology.* Minneapolis: Fortress, 1996.

Thomas, Mark G., Karl Skorecki, Haim Ben-Amid, Tudor Parfitt, Neil Bradman, and David B. Goldstein. "Origins of Old Testament Priests." *Nature* 394 no. 6689 (1998): 138–140.

Tomson, Peter. *Paul and the Jewish Law: Halakha in the Letters of the Apostle to the Gentiles.* Minneapolis: Fortress, 1990.

Tomson, Peter. *If This Be from Heaven: Jesus and the New Testament Authors in Their Relationship to Judaism.* Sheffield: Sheffield Academic Press, 2001.

Tucker, J. Brian. *Remain in Your Calling: Paul and the Continuation of Social Identities in 1 Corinthians.* Eugene, OR: Pickwick, 2011.

Weissman, Moshe. *The Midrash Says: On the Weekly Haftaros.* 5 vols. Brooklyn, NY: Bnay Yaakov Publications, 2003.

Wootten, Batya. *The Olive Tree of Israel.* White Stone, FL: House of David, 1992.

Wootten, Batya. *Who Is Israel? And Why You Need to Know.* Saint Cloud, FL: Key of David Publishing, 1998.

Wootten, Batya. "Law and Grace: A Love Story." Messianic Israel Alliance. No pages. Cited 14 February 2012. Online: http://www.messianicisrael.com/news/teachings/law-and-grace-a-love-story.html?Itemid=39.

Younger, Lawson K., Jr. "The Deportations of the Israelites." *Journal of Biblical Literature* 117 no. 2 (Summer 1998): 201–227.

Younger, Lawson K., Jr. "Israelites in Exile." *BAR* 29 no. 6 (Nov/Dec 2003): 36–45, 65–66.

Zetterholm, Magnus. *The Formation of Christianity in Antioch: A Social-Scientific Approach to the Separation between Judaism and Christianity.* New York: Routledge, 2003.

ENDNOTES

1   Zvi Ben-Dor Benite, *The Ten Lost Tribes: A World History* (Oxford: Oxford University Press, 2009), 23.

2   The speculative "may be" is used throughout this book, as many Two-House advocates are careful to note in their publications that there is no way to prove their hypothesis. However, one should note that the entire system of Two-House theology, including its name, is based on this hypothesis. If it is incorrect, the entire movement is superfluous. It is safe to assume that the theory of Israelite ancestry is widely accepted within the movement.

3   Unless otherwise noted, all Scripture quotations are taken from the English Standard Version.

4   The term "Gentile" here and throughout means nothing more than "non-Jew." The issue of Gentile identity being linked with paganism will be addressed in chapter four. For a detailed study on the term "Gentile," see Toby Janicki, "What Is a Gentile?" *Messiah Journal* 101 (Summer 2009): 38–45.

5   Batya Wootten, *Who Is Israel? And Why You Need To Know* (Saint Cloud, FL: Key of David Publishing, 1998), 13.

6   Wootten, *Who Is Israel?* 152–153.

7   Simon J. DeVries, *1 Kings* (2d ed.; vol. 12 of *Word Biblical Commentary;* Waco, TX: WORD, 1985), 151.

8   Or perhaps even four, if one counts Simeon (Joshua 19:9, cf. First Fruits of Zion's Torah Club Volume Three, 179, n. 7).

9   Cf. Ezra 1:5; Nehemiah 11.

10   Tudor Parfitt, *The Lost Tribes of Israel: The History of a Myth* (London: Phoenix, 2002), contains a comprehensive account of these different theories and their origins.

11   Parfitt, 106–111.

12   Mark Kinzer, *Postmissionary Messianic Judaism* (Grand Rapids: Brazos, 2005), 290.

13   Dan Cohn-Sherbok, *Messianic Judaism* (New York: Continuum, 2001), 58–59, 64–71.

14   Sandy Bloomfield, *The Errors of 'The Ephraimite Error'* (Lebanon, TN: Messianic Israel Alliance, 2008), 3. Cf. the membership application to the MJAA, available at their website, http://www.mjaa.org/.

15   Bloomfield, 4.

16   Nor, for that matter, do mainstream (non-Messianic) Jewish sources teach this. The Jewish people are called to be holy (distinct), not superior.

17   Boaz Michael, *Encounters with an Ephraimite* (unpublished white paper, 2003), 6.

18   This theological shift and the reasons for it are detailed in Boaz Michael and D. Thomas Lancaster, "One Law and the Messianic Gentile," *Messiah Journal* 101 (Summer 2009): 46-70.

19   Wootten's work is, by this time, dated. However, more refined developments of Two-House theology have not been widely accepted in the Two-House movement. Our summary of Two-House theology here is meant to reflect the popular understanding of said theology within the movement itself. Discussions of further developments, especially those of prolific Two-House writer J. K. McKee, are inevitably more technical and beyond the scope of this introductory work. However, in an effort to make this publication as relevant and up-to-date as possible, reflections on McKee's variant of Two-House theology will appear in the footnotes. Other popular Two-House teachers who primarily teach through audio format would be: Bill Cloud; Brad Scott; Daniel Botkin; Eddie Chumney; Rico Cortez; Tony Robinson; Scott Diffenderfer; and Jim Staley. While their works are not mentioned in this work, each of them espouse this doctrine to one degree or another.

20   Wootten, *Who Is Israel?* 74: "Israelites can be anywhere and have any and every ethnic look known to man."

21   Ibid.

22   Cf. Batya Wootten, *The Olive Tree of Israel* (White Stone, FL: House of David, 1992), 49: "Of necessity, these nations would primarily, but not exclusively, be located in the West."

23   Wootten, *Who Is Israel?* 153. Again, Wootten is careful not to dogmatically assert that Ephraimites are covenant-bound to every commandment of Torah, but the idea is implied: "Those claiming faith in the Messiah of the New Covenant would hear about the Law of Moses—and that the Holy Spirit would write the Law on their hearts. For that was the very heart of the promise! That was how Israel's divided kingdom would be restored!" Cf. Wootten, "Law and Grace:

A Love Story": "Once we see that man was created for good works, the question becomes: how can we know what are good works? We cannot know apart from the Instruction manual that is the Torah," n.p. [cited 14 February 2012]. Online: http://www.messianicisrael.com/news/teachings/law-and-grace-a-love-story.html?Itemid=39.

24 E.g., Jack Carstens, *Is the Church Ephraim?* (2d ed.; self-published in 2007), 7.

25 For a discussion of the biblical precedent for these practices see Toby Janicki, *Tefillin* (Marshfield, MO: First Fruits of Zion, 2011), and Aaron Eby, *Biblically Kosher* (Marshfield, MO: First Fruits of Zion, 2012).

26 J. K. McKee, "One Law for All" [cited 14 February 2012]. Online: http://tnnonline.net/torah/one-law/index.html. For a refutation of this exegesis of the "one-law" passages from the Torah see Toby Janicki, "One Law for All," *Messiah Journal* 105 (Fall 2010): 24–31.

27 Wootten, *Who Is Israel?* 197–203.

28 Wootten, *Who Is Israel?* 201; cf. Wootten, *Olive Tree*, 54.

29 Kay Silberling, "The Ephraimite Error" (position paper submitted to the International Messianic Jewish Alliance, 1999), 36.

30 For a biblical perspective on halachic authority see Tsvi Sadan, "Halachic Authority in the Life of the Messianic Community," *Messiah Journal* 109 (Winter 2012): 13–26, and Mark Kinzer, "Messianic Judaism and Jewish Tradition in the 21st Century: A Biblical Defense of 'Oral Torah'" (paper presented at the annual meeting of the Hashivenu conference, Pasadena, CA, 2003) [cited 14 February 2012]. Online: http://www.hashivenu.org/index.php?option=com_docman&task=doc_download&gid=39&Itemid=268.

31 Wootten, *Who Is Israel?* 184.

32 Wootten, *Who Is Israel?* 182. For a biblical defense of the Jewish Calendar see D. Thomas Lancaster, "Lunar Calendar and Aviv Barley" [cited 14 February 2012]. Online: http://ffoz.org/_php/download.php?file=Lunar-Calendar-and-Aviv-Barley.pdf.

33 Wootten, *Who Is Israel?* 97.

34 Wootten, *Who Is Israel?* 181.

35 Wootten, *Who Is Israel?* 185.

36 This term is borrowed from R. Kendall Soulen, *The God of Israel and Christian Theology* (Minneapolis: Fortress, 1996).

37 Wootten, *Who Is Israel?* 17.

38 Silberling, "Ephraimite Error," 2–4.

39 Wootten, *Who Is Israel?* 1–7.

40 Wootten, *Olive Tree*, 42.

41   Wootten, *Olive Tree,* 50.

42   See Torah Club Volume Three, 167–168 for a discussion of which tribes went where.

43   Lawson K. Younger, Jr., "The Deportations of the Israelites," *Journal of Biblical Literature* 117 no. 2 (Summer 1998): 216; quoted in Benite, *Ten Lost Tribes,* 33.

44   Magen Broshi and Israel Finkelstein, "The Population of Palestine in Iron Age II," *Bulletin of the American Schools of Oriental Research* 287 (1992): 47–60, quoted in Benite, 34.

45   Benite, *Ten Lost Tribes,* 34–35.

46   David Baron, *History of the Ten Lost Tribes: Anglo-Israelism Examined* (London: Morgan and Scott, 1915), 24–25.

47   Silberling, "Ephraimite Error," 11.

48   First Fruits of Zion's *Torah Club Volume Three,* 169.

49   Moshe Eisemann, *Yechezkel: A New Translation with a Commentary Anthologized from Talmudic, Midrashic, and Rabbinic Sources* (Brooklyn: Mesorah, 2009), 573.

50   Many, but not all; the fact that many did not assimilate and could still be identified as Jewish will be discussed below, along with the Epistle of James.

51   In contrast to the Two-House teaching that they were dispersed to the ends of the earth (a term that finds its roots in Assyrian propaganda; Benite, *Ten Lost Tribes,* 38–45). Lawson K. Younger, "Israelites in Exile," *BAR* 29 no. 6 (Nov/Dec 2003): "Probably the bulk of the Israelite deportees served as agricultural laborers organized into 'cohorts' ... In order to maximize farming productivity, the state forced the deportees into a socio-economic mold that promoted their assimilation—their Assyrianization. Not only can we account for the various deportations of the Israelites that took place in the period 734–715 B.C.E., but we can also trace the process of their assimilation into Assyrian culture. In this sense, the Israelites were never 'lost.' Though the legend of 'the Lost Tribes' continues to capture people's imaginations, archaeology has made it possible for us to understand what actually happened to this ancient diaspora."

52   Silberling, 8–10.

53   Notably, Silberling does not mention this passage even once, despite its centrality to Two-House theology.

54   Silberling, 10–15.

55   *Torah Club Volume Three,* 168.

56   "We do not believe that it is the job of any non-Jewish Believer to label himself or herself as a physical Israelite." J. K. McKee, "'The

Ephraimite Error': Critical Errors," 12 [cited 14 February 2012]. Online: http://tnnonline.net/israel/ee-ce/index.html.

57 "As a born again Believer, be you Jewish or non-Jewish, you are a part of the Commonwealth of Israel. As a part of Israel, you will be participating in the end-time prophecies that relate to Israel. This includes the regathering, reunification, and restoration of all Israel, including the scattered Northern Kingdom." J. K. McKee, "Cross-Examining the Two-House Teaching," 4 [cited 14 February 2012]. Online: http://tnnonline.net/israel/cross-examining-2house/index. html.

58 Baron, 28.

59 Acts 14:1, 18:4, 19:10, 19:17, 20:21; Romans 1:16, 2:10, 3:9, 3:29, 9:24, 10:12; 1 Corinthians 1:22, 10:32, 12:13; Galatians 2:15, 3:28; Colossians 3:11.

60 Silberling, 19.

61 Mark 7:24–30 (also Matthew 15:21–28), Matthew 8:5–13 (also Luke 7:1–10), and John 4, all of which serve to highlight the distinction Jesus drew between Jew and Gentile.

62 So argues Silberling, 19.

63 Cf. Torah Club Volume Four, 626.

64 So argues Wootten, *Who Is Israel?*, 153-54.

65 *Revelation 17–22* (Nashville: Thomas Nelson, 1998), 1154.

66 *The Book of Revelation* (Grand Rapids: Eerdmans, 1998), 390-91.

67 The ritual of circumcision was not just a matter of outpatient surgery. Mark Nanos lucidly describes the scholarly consensus in this area in *The Irony of Galatians: Paul's Letter in First-Century Context* (Minneapolis: Fortress, 1996), 86–102. Circumcision in the New Testament is shorthand for "proselyte conversion," the process by which one became Jewish.

68 For example, Peter Davids, *The Epistle of James* (Grand Rapids: Eerdmans, 1982), 63.

69 Scot McKnight, *The Letter of James* (Grand Rapids: Eerdmans, 2011), 67: "[For James, the term] 'twelve tribes' is both messianic and still ethno-religiously inseparable from the Jewish community." Cf. Douglas Moo, *The Letter of James* (Grand Rapids: Eerdmans, 2000), 49–50.

70 McKnight, 66.

71 Richard Bauckham, *James* (New York: Routledge, 1999), 15.

72 Wootten, *Who Is Israel?* 35–40.

73 *Antiquities* XI.5.2.

74   4 Ezra 13:40–47, in *Apocalyptic Literature and Testaments* (vol. 1 of *The Old Testament Pseudepigrapha* , James H. Charlesworth ed.; New York: Doubleday, 1983), 552–553.

75   Richard Bauckham, *Gospel Women: Studies of the Named Women in the Gospels* (Grand Rapids: Eerdmans, 2002), 101.

76   As stated above, the ten tribes assimilated into the Jewish people long before the time of the Amoraim.

77   y.*Sanhedrin* 29b, *Genesis Rabbah* 73:5; cited in Parfitt, 7.

78   Baron, 45.

79   Moshe Weissman, *The Midrash Says—On the Weekly Haftaros*, vol. 1 (Brooklyn, NY: Bnay Yaakov Publications, 2003), 358, citing Rashi and *Midrash Shocher Tov.*

80   Wootten, *Who Is Israel?* 4.

81   Karl Skorecki et al., "Y Chromosomes of Jewish Priests," *Nature* 385 no. 6611 (1997): 32.

82   Mark G. Thomas et al., "Origins of Old Testament Priests," *Nature* 394 no. 6689 (1998): 138–140.

83   Gil Atzmon et al., "Abraham's Children in the Genome Era: Major Jewish Diaspora Populations Comprise Distinct Genetic Clusters with Shared Middle Eastern Ancestry," *American Journal of Human Genetics* 86 no. 6 (2010): 850–859; Doron Behar et al., "The Genome-Wide Structure of the Jewish People," *Nature* 466 no. 7303 (2010): 238–242.

84   Cf. Genesis 17:14.

85   Wootten, *Who Is Israel?* 97.

86   Notably, the four-letter name of God does not appear even once in the New Testament, though it would have been relatively easy to transliterate into Greek. Apparently the New Testament authors followed Jewish tradition by substituting for God's name circumlocutions such as *theos* (God), *kurios* (Lord), and *ouranos* (Heaven). For further information, see Aaron Eby and Toby Janicki, *Hallowed Be Your Name* (Marshfield, MO: First Fruits of Zion, 2008).

87   Wootten, *Who Is Israel?* 4.

88   J. K. McKee, "Cross-examining," 1: "All believe that non-Jewish Believers through faith in Messiah Yeshua are a part of the community of Israel, *the same as any Jewish person*" (emphasis mine).

89   Daniel Lancaster, *The Holy Epistle to the Galatians* (Marshfield, MO: First Fruits of Zion, 2011), 188–195.

90   Jack Carstens, *Is the Church Ephraim?* 77.

91   Magnus Zetterholm details the result of the Jewish community's rejection of similar claims made by early Christians in his book *The*

Formation of Christianity in Antioch: A Social-Scientific Approach to the Separation between Judaism and Christianity (New York: Routledge, 2003). He postulates that early Christian anti-Jewish writers such as Ignatius were motivated by Jewish rejection of Christian claims, though Christians were initially sympathetic to the Jewish people. The parallels between Zetterholm's model, the reaction of Luther to Jewish rejection of his claims, and the reaction of many Hebrew roots advocates toward Judaism and the Jewish people are uncanny.

92   Silberling, 31–34.

93   Some Two-House advocates, like J. K. McKee, recognize the potential for anti-Semitism in the movement and have laudably tried to head off this type of thinking. See his 2011 monograph, "Anti-Semitism in the Two-House Movement." His corrections to some of the worst offenses of the Two-House movement are significant, wide-ranging, and refreshing. However, one wonders whether some of the issues he is trying to correct are natural consequences of Two-House theology. McKee claims that a "wider restoration of Israel" is compatible with a Messianic Judaism that preserves and protects Jewish tradition and identity, yet he gives no solution to the problem of non-Jews overwhelming Jews in Messianic synagogues. He advocates respect toward Judaism and the synagogue, but does not address the fact that claiming to have a status equal to that of the Jewish people is inherently disrespectful to Judaism. He claims to respect Jewish tradition, but disregards the fact that Jewish tradition applies only to Jews and is inseparable from the Jewish community itself. At its core, his position is not different from the one we are arguing against here.

94   Herbert W. Armstrong, *The United States and Britain in Prophecy* (published without copyright, 1945).

95   The most popular being Steven M. Collins, *The "Lost" Ten Tribes of Israel ... Found!* (Boring, OR: CPA Books, 1995).

96   McKee admits as much in "'The Ephraimite Error': Critical Errors," 33 [cited 14 February 2012]. Online: http://tnnonline.net/israel/ee-ce/index.html.

97   See for example *Joseph: The Israelite Destiny of America* (Jerusalem: Brit-Am, 2001; repr. Russell-Davis, 2005), 21, in which he equates the English word "British" with the Hebrew words "Brit" (covenant) and "Ish" (man), an etymology not supported by modern scholarship. See Silberling, 25.

98   McKee expresses considerable concern over this development and advocates a Two-House theology that does not identify the descendants of Ephraim *at all, with any certainty* ("'The Ephraimite Error': Critical Errors," 12). Again, one wonders what the value of

Two-House theology is with no Ephraimites. How can there be a "wider restoration of Israel" before the Messiah comes if there are no Ephraimites to take part in it? By shifting the focus of Two-House theology from ethnic status to allegedly unfulfilled prophecy, McKee takes all of the wind out of the movement's sails. Yet his *practical* focus—being accepted as a full-fledged (undifferentiated?) part of Judaism despite not being Jewish—does not hinge on unfulfilled prophecy but on status, and is essentially the same focus as that of other Two-House proponents. Cf. J. K. McKee, "A Place Where Everyone Can Belong," 1 [cited 14 February 2012]. Online: http://tnnonline.net/messianic-issues/everyone-belong/index.html: "The battle for the 2010s is going to be about how every Believer can be included in the Messianic movement ... I know that I have not really found a [Messianic Jewish congregation] to date where I have truly felt that *my needs* have been met" (italics in original).

99   Baron, 52–53 (italics mine).

100 *A Dictionary of Jewish-Christian Relations*, eds. Edward Kessler and Neil Wenborn (Cambridge: Cambridge University Press, 2005), s.v. "Supersessionism."

101 On Jeremiah 31:31–34, see for example Walter Brueggemann, *A Commentary on Jeremiah: Exile and Homecoming* (Grand Rapids: Eerdmans, 1998), 291–292: "This oracle of promise ... has frequently been preempted by Christians in a supersessionist fashion, as though Jews belong to the old covenant now nullified and Christians are the sole heirs of the new covenant ... Such a preemptive reading ignores the text itself. Moreover, such a rendering of the future could hardly be expected or cogent in the midst of these several promissory oracles which anticipate the reconstitution of the Israelite community. Such a supersessionist reading in fact asserts the rejection rather than the reconstitution of Israel, a point not on the horizon of these oracles." On Romans 11, Douglas Moo, *The Epistle to the Romans* (Grand Rapids: Eerdmans, 1996), 721, writes that Paul "counters a tendency for Gentiles to appropriate for themselves exclusively the rights and titles of 'God's people.'" Brendan Byrne, *Romans* (Collegeville, MN: Liturgical Press, 1996), 344, writes: "Far from any 'replacement' view of Christianity with respect to Judaism, Paul cannot think of the salvation of believers apart from the restoration of the original stock."

102 R. Kendall Soulen traces its development from Irenaeus and Justin Martyr through the Enightenment and on to Barth and Rahner in *The God of Israel and Christian Theology* (Minneapolis, MN: Fortress, 1996), 1–106.

103 Silberling, 20.

104 Justin Howell, "The Imperial Authority and Benefaction of Centurions and Acts 10.34–43," *JSNT* 31, no. 1 (2008): 33–36.

105 Lancaster, *Galatians*, 31–32 and Toby Janicki, "We Are the God-Fearers," *Messiah Journal* 103 (Spring 2010): 33–38.

106 Paula Fredricksen, *Augustine and the Jews* (New York: Doubleday, 2008), 3–40, 88–90.

107 Acts 10:2 records that he prayed continually; v. 30 records that he was praying at the ninth hour (around 3 p.m.), identified in Acts 3:1 as the "hour of prayer"—the afternoon sacrifice, today called the *Minchah* prayer. Cf. Torah Club Volume Six, 224–225.

108 David Rudolph, *A Jew to the Jews* (Tübingen: Mohr Siebeck, 2011), 35–49, details the finer points of *koinos* as well as the importance of the meanings of both words for interpreting Peter's vision.

109 See Eby, *Biblically Kosher*, 40–47.

110 According to one chronology of Paul's life, Galatians (including 5:19–21, which prohibits idolatry) was written around 47 CE to the churches in Asia Minor to whom he had just finished ministering, so this must have been a stance Paul took from the beginning (cf. Ronald Fung, *The Epistle to the Galatians* [Grand Rapids: Eerdmans, 1988], 9–28). Even if this chronology is incorrect, and 1 Thessalonians is the earliest of Paul's letters, 1 Thessalonians 1:9 confirms that Paul's Gentile converts turned away from idols; i.e., they quit their involvement in the various cults which Roman law required them to be involved in.

111 Toby Janicki, "What Is a Gentile?" *Messiah Journal* 101 (Spring 2009): 42: "Peter's experience with Cornelius ... serves as a *ma'aseh* (מעשה), i.e., a ruling on *halachah* based on the occurrence of an actual event, that permits entering the houses of and eating with the uncircumcised believers in Yeshua."

112 Baron, 35: "The name of 'Jew' and 'Israelite' became synonymous terms from about the time of the Captivity. It is one of the absurd fallacies of Anglo-Israelism to presuppose that the term 'Jew' stands for a bodily descendant of 'Judah.' It stands for all those from among the sons of Jacob who acknowledged themselves, or were considered, subjects of the theocratic kingdom of Judah." Cf. Peter Tomson, *If This Be from Heaven: Jesus and the New Testament Authors in Their Relationship to Judaism* (Sheffield: Sheffield Academic Press, 2001), 112–113.

113 The one possible exception, Ephesians 2:12, will be discussed below.

114 Janicki, "What Is a Gentile?" 43: "In apostolic vernacular, Gentiles are still called Gentiles even after coming to Messiah, yet at the same time the connotation of 'pagan' is sometimes retained in the context. This

creates a difficult dichotomy in definition, but it is one with which the apostles were comfortable operating."

115 Fredricksen, xx.

116 Janicki, "What Is a Gentile," 38–45.

117 Romans 11:13; Galatians 2:8.

118 Philip Esler, *Conflict and Identity in Romans* (Minneapolis: Fortress, 2003), 38.

119 Minna Shkul, *Reading Ephesians: Exploring Social Entrepreneurship in the Text* (New York: T&T Clark, 2010), xi.

120 J. Brian Tucker, *Remain in Your Calling* (Eugene, OR: Pickwick, 2011), 33–61.

121 A fairly comprehensive study of these idioms is available in Brenda B. Colijn, *Images of Salvation in the New Testament* (Downers Grove, IL: IVP Academic, 2010).

122 Lancaster, *Galatians*, 187–196.

123 Tucker, 119.

124 Tucker, 129.

125 Nevertheless, Paul and the apostles make heavy use of the Torah and even of Jewish traditional categories of law to inform Gentile obligations to God. See Toby Janicki, "The Gentile Believer's Obligation to the Torah of Moses," *Messiah Journal* 109 (Winter 2012): 45–62; also Peter Tomson, *Paul and the Jewish Law* (Minneapolis: Fortress, 1990), and Markus Bockmuehl, *Jewish Law in Gentile Churches* (Edinburgh: T&T Clark, 2000). A distinction must be made between the Torah as a covenant between God and Israel and the Torah as a source for determining *halachah* for other people groups.

126 Tucker (115–135) uses the term "microidentity" to describe the differentiation between Jew and Gentile in the body of Christ. While Tucker acknowledges that Paul argued for unity in the body of Christ, he also argues from 1 Corinthians that Jews and Gentiles retained their respective microidentities; Jews observed the Torah, and Gentiles a more general set of laws that are drawn from the Torah's instructions for the "sojourner." Within the unified *ecclesia* (assembly, "church"), there was variegation. For support, Tucker cites Mark Nanos, *The Mystery of Romans* (Minneapolis: Fortress, 1996), 50–56 and Peter Tomson, *Paul and the Jewish Law*, 19, 23, 220, and 269, both of which are excellent sources for further study in this area. Also see Janicki, "The Gentile Believer's Obligation," which argues that the Gentile believers were (and still are) obligated to nearly all of the commandments—far more than just the laws for sojourners or Noachides (righteous Gentiles).

127 James Dunn, *The Theology of Paul the Apostle* (Grand Rapids: Eerdmans, 1998), 227–228.

128 George Eldon Ladd, *A Theology of the New Testament* (Grand Rapids: Eerdmans, 1993), 524–525.

129 Dunn, 329.

130 Dunn, 328–323; cf. Colijn, *Images.*

131 Tucker, *Remain in Your Calling*, 127–135, deals with arguments that though the believing Gentiles are never called Israel, nevertheless they are implied to be so.

132 Andrew Lincoln, *Ephesians* (Waco, TX: Word, 1990), 137.

133 David Rudolph, "The Relationship Between the Church and Israel," *Verge* 2 no. 2 (2010): 4.

134 Tucker, 33–61.

135 David Rudolph, *A Jew to the Jews*, 45–46, explains Philippians 3 in this light.

136 "The Gentile Believer's Obligation to the Torah of Moses," 45–62.